ABIDING INK

Publisher's note:
This modern version has been updated from the complete original text. Words, expressions, and sentence structure have been revised for clarity and readability.

All rights are reserved. No part of this revised text may be reproduced or distributed without the publisher's explicit written consent.

AbidingInk.org

COME AND WELCOME TO JESUS CHRIST

John Bunyan (1681)
Revised To Modern English (2025)

A Plain and Profitable Discourse on John 6:37. This work shows the cause, truth, and manner of a sinner's coming to Jesus Christ, along with his joyful reception and blessed welcome.

1.	Introduction	4
2.	The Text Explained	8
3.	The Father: Giver of the Gift	12
4.	The Father's Purpose in Giving	16
5.	The Son: Receiver of the Gift	20
6.	What It Means to Come to Christ	21
7.	The Promise's Power to Draw People to Christ	40
8.	Christ's Promise to All Who Come to Him	61
9.	Two Kinds of Sinners Who Come to Christ	74
10.	What It Means to Be Rejected by Christ	88
11.	Christ's Power to Save or Reject	96
12.	Key Observations from the Text	100
13.	We Cannot Come Unless the Father Draws Us	102
14.	Many Who Come to Christ Fear He Won't Accept Them	116
15.	Fear of Not Coming to Christ Fast Enough	135
16.	Christ Wants No One Who Comes to Fear Rejection	143
17.	Reasons for the Observation	146
18.	Practical Application	149

1. Introduction

"All that the Father gives Me shall come to Me, and the one who comes to Me I will by no means cast out." - John 6:37

A little earlier in John chapter 6, you can read that the Lord Jesus walked on the sea to go to Capernaum after sending His disciples ahead in a boat. However, the wind was contrary, which hindered the ship's passage. Around the fourth watch of the night, Jesus came walking on the sea and overtook them, causing them to be afraid at the sight of Him.

Note that when providences are dark and frightening for God's people, the Lord Jesus reveals Himself to them in wonderful ways. Sometimes, they can bear this revelation as little as they can bear the things that were previously terrifying to them. They were afraid of the wind and the waves; they were also afraid of their Lord and Savior when He appeared to them in that state.

But He said, "Do not be afraid; it is I."

Note that the purpose of the Lord Jesus appearing to His people, even when the manner of His appearance is terrifying, is to calm their fears and anxieties.

Then they received Him into the ship, and immediately the ship was at the land where they were going.

Note that when Christ is absent from His people, they progress slowly and with great difficulty. However, when He joins them, oh, how quickly they steer their course! How soon they reach their destination!

The people among whom He last preached, when they saw that both Jesus and His disciples were gone, also took a boat and went to Capernaum, seeking Jesus. When they found Him, they asked in wonder, "Rabbi, when did You come here?" But the Lord Jesus, disregarding their compliment, answered, "Most assuredly, I say to you, you seek Me, not because you saw the miracles, but because you ate of the loaves and were filled."

Note that people may follow Christ for base reasons, as these did when they pursued Him across the sea for loaves. A person's appetite can drive them a long way in religion; indeed, a person's hunger can make them go to great lengths for Christ.

Note again, they are not feigning compliments, but rather expressing gracious intentions, which crown the work in the eyes of Christ. It is not the toil and business of professors, but their love for Him that makes Him approve of them.

Note again, when people look for friendly reception from Christ, if their hearts are corrupt, they will encounter a rebuke. "You seek Me, not because you saw the miracles, but because you ate of the loaves and were filled."

Yet observe again, He does not refuse to give good counsel, even to those who come with insincere intentions. He urges them to labor for the food that endures to eternal life. Oh! how willingly would Jesus Christ have even those professors, who come to Him with pretenses, come to Him sincerely so that they may be saved.

The text you will find is, after much more discussion with and about this people, a conclusion uttered by the Lord Jesus. It indicates that, since they were merely pretenders to faith and therefore not those in whom His soul could delight, He would be content with a remnant that His Father had given to Him.

In other words, He is saying, "I am not likely to be honored in your salvation; but the Father has given me a people, and they shall come to Me in truth, and in them will I find satisfaction."

Thus, the text may be referred to as Christ's repose. In fulfilling this, He rests content after much labor and many sermons spent, as it were, in vain. As He says through the prophet, "I have labored in vain, I have spent my strength for naught, and in vain" (Isaiah 49:4).

But as there He says, "My judgment is with the LORD, and My work with My God," so in the text He states, "All that the Father gives Me shall come to Me; and the one who comes to Me I will by no means cast out." Through these words, the Lord Jesus comforts Himself in light of the dissimulation of some of His followers. He also finds rest in considering the little effect His ministry had in Capernaum, Chorazin, and Bethsaida: "I thank You, O Father," He said, "Lord of heaven and earth, because You have hidden these things from the wise and prudent, and have revealed them to babes; even so, Father, for so it seemed good in Your sight" (Matthew 11:25; Luke 10:21).

The text, in general, consists of two parts and has special reference to the Father and the Son, as well as to their joint management of the salvation of the people: "All that the Father gives Me shall come to Me; and the one who comes to Me I will by no means cast out." The first part of the text clearly pertains to the Father and His gift; the other part relates to the Son and His reception of that gift.

Regarding the gift of the Father, we must consider the gift itself, which is the gift of certain persons to the Son. The Father gives, and that gift shall come: "And the one who comes." The gift, then, is of persons; the Father gives persons to Jesus Christ.

Next we have the Son's reception of this gift, which is evident in the following particulars:

1. In His heartfelt acknowledgment of it as a gift: "The Father gives Me."

2. In His solemn recognition of all and every part of the gift: "All that the Father gives Me."

3. In His resolution to bring them to Himself: "All that the Father gives Me shall come to Me."

4. And in His determination that nothing shall cause Him to reject them in their coming: "And the one who comes to Me I will by no means cast out."

These points could be elaborated upon at length, as they are presented in this method; however, I shall choose to address the words, First, by way of explication. Second, by way of observation.

2. The Text Explained

"All that the Father gives Me." The word "all" is often used in Scripture and should be understood in a broader or narrower sense, depending on the context. To better grasp the meaning of Christ's words here, we must recognize that it is specifically limited to those who will be saved, namely, those who will come to Christ; those whom He will "in no wise cast out."

Similarly, the phrase "all Israel" is sometimes used to refer to the entire family of Jacob. For example, "And so all Israel shall be saved" (Romans 11:26). Here, "all Israel" does not mean every individual in the broadest sense; "for they are not all Israel who are of Israel;" "nor are they all children because they are the seed of Abraham; but, 'In Isaac your seed shall be called.' That is, those who are the children of the flesh, these are not the children of God; but the children of the promise are counted as the seed" (Romans 9:6-8).

This word "all," therefore, must be interpreted both broadly and narrowly, depending on the truth and argument for which it is used; otherwise, we risk misusing Scripture, misleading readers, and deceiving ourselves. "And I, if I am lifted up from the earth," said Christ, "will draw all men to Myself" (John 12:32).

Can anyone truly believe that "all" in this context refers to every individual in the world, rather than those who align with the purpose of the passage? If being "lifted up from the earth" refers to His ascension into heaven, and if "drawing all men" means drawing them to that place of glory, then "all men" must refer specifically to those who will indeed be eternally saved from the coming wrath.

"For God has concluded them all in unbelief, that He might have mercy upon all" (Romans 11:32). Here again, we see two uses of "all," but with a significant difference between the first and second instances. The first "all" refers to the Jews, while the second "all" refers only to those among them upon whom God will have mercy. Thus, the "all" in our text must also be limited to those who are saved.

Furthermore, the word "gives" or "has given" must similarly be restricted to this limited number. "All that the Father gives Me." Not all that are given, if we consider the Father's gift to the Son in the broadest sense; for in that sense, many are given to Him who will never come to Him; indeed, many are given to Him whom He will "cast out." Therefore, I will first demonstrate the truth of this, and then clarify in what sense the gift in the text should be understood.

First, it is evident that "all" cannot be intended in its broadest sense. If "all" were meant to include everyone given to Christ, then all men, indeed, all things in the world, would have to be saved. "All things," He says, "have been delivered to Me by My Father" (Matthew 11:27). No rational person would conclude this. Therefore, the gift referred to in the text must be specifically limited to a select group given by the Father to the Son.

It must not be understood as "all" in any sense of those given by the Father to Him, because the Father has given some, indeed many, to Him to be destroyed. "Ask of Me," said the Father to Him, "and I will give You the nations for Your inheritance, and the ends of the earth for Your possession." But what will happen to them? Must He save them all? No. "You shall break them with a rod of iron; You shall dash them to pieces like a potter's vessel" (Psalm 2).

This approach is not used with those whom He saves by His grace, but with those whom He and the saints will rule over in justice and severity (Revelation 2:26, 27). Yet, as you see, "they are given to Him." Therefore, the gift referred to in the text must be limited to a specific group, given by the Father to the Son.

In Psalm 18, it is clearly stated that some are given to Him so that He might destroy them. "You have given me the necks of my enemies, that I might destroy those who hate me" (verse 40). Therefore, these cannot be included among those said to be given in the text; for those, even all of them, shall come to Him, "and He will in no wise cast them out."

Some are given to Christ so that He might accomplish some of His great and profound purposes in the world. For instance, Judas was given to Christ, so that through him, as was predetermined, He might bring about His death, and thus the salvation of His elect through His blood. Moreover, Judas had to manage this situation in such a way that he would ultimately lose himself forever in the process. Therefore, the Lord Jesus, even in the loss of Judas, must refer to the judgment of His Father, questioning whether He had done right in allowing Judas to bring about His own death, which was predetermined, leading to his own eternal damnation.

"Those," He said, "whom You gave Me, I have kept, and none of them is lost except the son of perdition; that the Scripture might be fulfilled" (John 17:12). Let us acknowledge that Judas was given to Christ, but not in the same manner as others are given to Him, not as those mentioned in the text; for then he would have failed to be received by Christ and kept for eternal life.

Indeed, he was given to Christ, but he was given to be lost, as I have previously mentioned; he was given to Christ so that through him, He might bring about His own death, as was determined beforehand, and in the downfall of Judas himself. He must fulfill the Scripture in his destruction, just as much as in the salvation of the others. "And none of them is lost, but the son of perdition; that the Scripture might be fulfilled."

The gift, therefore, in the text must not be taken in the broadest sense, but rather as the words allow, specifically as a gift that He accepts and promises to be an effective means of eternal salvation. "All that the Father gives Me shall come to Me; and him who comes to Me I will in no wise cast out."

Note! Those who are specially given to Me shall come, and they shall by no means be rejected. This is the essence of the text.

Thus, those intended as the gift in the text are those given to the Son by covenant; those referred to in other passages as "the elect," "the chosen," "the sheep," and "the children of the promise," etc. These are the ones that the Father has given to Christ to keep; those whom Christ has promised eternal life; those to whom He has given His word, and whom He will have with Him in His kingdom to behold His glory.

"This is the Father's will which has sent Me, that of all which He has given Me I should lose nothing, but should raise it up again at the last day" (John 6:39). "And I give unto them eternal life; and they shall never perish, neither shall anyone pluck them out of My hand. My Father who gave them to Me is greater than all; and no one is able to pluck them out of My Father's hand" (John 10:28). "As You have given Him power over all flesh, that He should give eternal life to as many as You have given Him. They were Yours, and You gave them to Me, and they have kept Your word; I pray for them: I do not pray for the world, but for those whom You have given Me; for they are Yours. And all Mine are Yours, and Yours are Mine; and I am glorified in them." "Keep through Your own name those whom You have given Me, that they may be one, as We are." "Father, I desire that they also, whom You have given Me, be with Me where I am; that they may behold My glory, which You have given Me; for You loved Me before the foundation of the world" (John 17:1, 6, 9, 10, 24).

All these statements convey the same meaning as the text; the terms "all" and "many," as well as "those," "they," etc., in these various sayings of Christ, refer to all those given in the text: "All that the Father gives." As I mentioned earlier, the word "ALL," along with other terms, must not be interpreted according to our misguided notions or unfounded opinions. Instead, it should allow for both expansion and limitation, in accordance with the true meaning and intent of the text. Therefore, we must diligently seek to understand the text by comparing it with other sayings of God. This will enable us to better discern the mind of the Lord through the word He has provided for us to know Him.

3. The Father: Giver of the Gift

"All that the Father gives." By using the term "Father," Christ identifies the person who gives; from this, we can learn several important things.

First, the Lord God, and Father of our Lord Jesus Christ, is involved with the Son in the salvation of His people. While His actions regarding our salvation differ from those of the Son—He did not die or shed blood for our redemption as the Son did—He still plays a significant role in our salvation. As Christ states, "The Father Himself loves you," and His love is evident in choosing us and giving us to His Son. Furthermore, He also gave His Son to be a ransom for us. Hence, He is called "The Father of mercies, and the God of all comfort." For it is through the Father that grace comes to us, through the wounds and the heart-blood of His beloved Son (Colossians 1:12-14). Therefore, we should remember and honor the Father as the one who has a primary role in the salvation of sinners. We ought to give "thanks unto the Father, who has made us meet to be partakers of the inheritance of the saints in light" (Colossians 1:12). For "the Father sent the Son to be the Savior of the world" (John 4:14). As we see in the text, the "Father gives" the sinner to Christ to save him.

Second, Christ Jesus the Lord, by using the term "Father," seeks to make this giver more familiar to us. Naturally, the name of God can be intimidating, especially when He is revealed through names that emphasize His justice, holiness, power, and glory. However, the term "Father" is a familiar word that does not frighten the sinner but rather inclines his heart to love and cherish the thought of Him. Thus, when Christ teaches us to pray with confidence, He instructs us to use the word "Father," saying, "When you pray, say, Our Father who art in heaven." This implies that through such familiarity, the children of God may feel bolder to pray for and request great things. I have often found that simply saying the word "Father" brings me more comfort than calling Him by any other name in Scripture. It is worth noting that referring to God by this relational title was rare among the saints in Old

Testament times. You seldom find Him called by this name; sometimes not even in three or four books. But now, in New Testament times, He is referred to by this name more than any other, both by the Lord Jesus Himself and by the apostles afterward. Indeed, the Lord Jesus was the one who first made this name common among the saints and taught them to use it frequently in their conversations, prayers, and writings. This name is more pleasing and clearly expresses our relationship with God than any other term; for through this one name, we understand that all our blessings are the result of God's grace and that we, who are called, are His children by adoption.

Note the importance of the word "gives"- "All that the Father gives."

The word "gives" is somewhat outside of Christ's usual language and seems to suggest, at first glance, that the Father's gift to the Son is not merely a past act but one that is ongoing and continuous. In reality, this gift was bestowed upon Christ when the eternal covenant was established between them before the foundation of the world. Therefore, in other instances where this gift is mentioned, it is referred to as a past act, such as "All that He has given Me; to as many as You have given Me; You gave them to Me; and those whom You have given Me." Thus, this must be the primary and essential meaning of the text regarding this word "gives." Otherwise, the doctrine of election and the eternal covenant made between the Father and the Son, in which this gift is certainly included, would be undermined or at least questioned by erroneous and wicked individuals. They might argue that the Father did not give all those who will be saved to Christ before the world was created, as this act of giving appears to be one of continuation. However, this word "gives" should not be dismissed, for it has its proper significance. It may indicate to us that while the act of giving among humans can refer to past or future time, with God, it is not so. Past and future events are always present to God and to His Son Jesus Christ. He "calls those things which do not exist as though they did" (Romans 4:17). Furthermore, "Known to God are all His works from the beginning of the world." All things are present to God, and thus the gift of the Father to the Son, although it appears to us as a past act (Acts 15:16), is indeed always present.

Christ may express Himself in this way to indicate that the Father has not only given Him this portion in the lump before the world was created, but that those whom He has given will also be brought to Him at the time of their conversion. For the Father brings them to Christ (John 6:44). As it is said, "She shall be brought to the king in garments of needlework," which signifies being clothed in the righteousness of Christ; for it is God who imputes that righteousness to those who are saved (Psalm 45:14; 1 Corinthians 1). A father gives his daughter to a man in marriage, which refers to a past act, and he gives her again at the appointed time of the wedding. In this latter sense, perhaps the text may have a deeper meaning: that all whom the Father has given to Jesus Christ before the world was created, He gives again to Him at the day of their espousals.

Gifts given among men are often best when they are new; that is, when they are first received. This is because all earthly things grow old. However, with Christ, it is not so. This gift from the Father is not old, worn out, or unpleasant in His sight; therefore, it is always new to Him. When the Lord spoke of giving the land of Canaan to the Israelites, He did not say that He had given or would give it to them, but rather: "The Lord your God gives you this good land" (Deuteronomy 9:6). This does not mean that He had not given it to them while they were still in the loins of their fathers hundreds of years earlier. Yet He states that He gives it to them now, as if they were in the very act of taking possession, even though they were still on the other side of the Jordan. What, then, should be the meaning? I believe it signifies this: that the land should always feel new to them, as if they were taking possession of it for the first time. Likewise, the gift of the Father mentioned in the text is always new, as if it were perpetually fresh.

"All that the Father gives Me." In these words, we see mention of two persons: the Father and the Son. The Father is the giver, and the Son is the one who receives or accepts this gift. This clearly demonstrates that the Father and the Son, though they, along with the Holy Spirit, are one eternal God, are distinct in their personalities. The Father is one, the Son is one, and the Holy Spirit is one.

Since this text only mentions two of the three, let us focus on these two. The giver and the receiver cannot be the same person in the act of giving and receiving. He who gives does not give to himself but to another. The Father does not give to the Father, that is, to Himself, but to the Son. The Son does not receive from the Son, that is, from Himself, but from the Father. When the Father gives a commandment, He does not give it to Himself but to another. As Christ says, "He gave Me a commandment" (John 12:49). Again, He states, "I am one who bears witness of Myself, and the Father who sent Me bears witness of Me" (John 8:18).

Furthermore, there is something implied that is not explicitly stated: the Father has not given all men to Christ. In the context of this text, although He has given every one of them in a broader sense, if He had given all, then all would be saved. Therefore, He has disposed of some in another way. He gives some over to idolatry; He gives some up to uncleanness, vile affections, and a reprobate mind. He disposes of these in His anger for their destruction, allowing them to reap the consequences of their actions and be filled with the reward of their own ways (Acts 7:42; Romans 1:24, 26, 28).

However, He has not disposed of all men in this manner. In mercy, He has reserved some from these judgments, and those are the ones He will pardon, as He says, "For I will pardon those whom I reserve" (Jeremiah 50:20). These are the ones He has given to Jesus Christ as a legacy and portion. Hence, the Lord Jesus says, "This is the Father's will which has sent Me, that of all whom He has given Me, I should lose nothing, but should raise it up again at the last day" (John 6:39).

4. The Father's Purpose in Giving

The Father, therefore, in giving them to Him to save them, must declare the following things:

1. He is able to fulfill this divine purpose of saving them to the uttermost, through sin, temptation, and so forth (Hebrews 7:25). Hence, He is described as laying "help upon one who is mighty," "mighty to save" (Psalm 89:19; Isaiah 63:1). God has even promised from ancient times to send His people "a Savior, a great one" (Isaiah 19:20).

To save is a great work that requires almightiness in the one undertaking it. Therefore, He is called the "Mighty God, the Wonderful Counselor," and so forth. Sin is strong, Satan is also strong, death and the grave are strong, as is the curse of the law. Thus, it follows that this Jesus must be accounted almighty by God the Father, as He has given His elect to Him to save them and deliver them from these forces, despite all their strength and power.

He demonstrated this might when He was engaged in that part of our deliverance that required a declaration of it. He abolished death; He destroyed him who had the power of death; He vanquished the grave; He finished sin and put an end to its damning effects upon those the Father has given Him. He triumphed over the curse of the law, nailing it to His cross, and openly displayed His victory (2 Timothy 1:10; Hebrews 2:14-15; Hosea 13:14; Daniel 9:24; Galatians 3:13; Colossians 2:14-15).

Even now, as a sign of His triumph and conquest, He is alive from the dead and holds the keys of hell and death in His own keeping (Revelation 1:18).

2. The Father's giving them to Him to save them declares that He is and will be faithful in His office as Mediator. Therefore, they shall be secured from the consequences and wages of their sins, which is eternal

damnation, through His faithful execution of this role. Indeed, it is said, even by the Holy Spirit, that He "was faithful to Him who appointed Him," that is, to the work of saving those the Father has given Him for this purpose; just as "Moses was faithful in all his house."

Yet, He is more faithful than Moses, for Moses was faithful in God's house only as a servant; "but Christ as a Son over His own house" (Hebrews 3). Therefore, this man is counted worthy of more glory than Moses, not only because of His faithfulness but also due to the dignity of His person. In Him, and in His truth and faithfulness, God rests well pleased and has placed all the governance of His people upon His shoulders.

Knowing that nothing will be lacking in Him that may perfect this design, the Son has already provided proof of this. When the time came for His blood to be required by Divine justice for their redemption, washing, and cleansing, He poured it out freely from His heart, as if it were water from a vessel. He did not hesitate to part with His own life so that the life laid up for His people in heaven would not fail to be bestowed upon them. For this reason, as well as others, God calls Him "My righteous servant" (Isaiah 53:11). His righteousness could never have been complete if He had not been utterly faithful to the work He undertook. It is also because He is faithful and true that He judges and works for His people's deliverance in righteousness. He will faithfully fulfill this trust placed in Him. The Father knows this and has therefore given His elect to Him.

3. The Father's giving them to Him to save them declares that He is and will be gentle and patient with them under all their provocations and failures. It is unimaginable the trials and provocations that the Son of God has faced with these people He saves. Indeed, He is called "a tried stone," for He has been tested not only by the devil, the guilt of sin, death, and the curse of the law, but also by His people's ignorance, unruliness, falls into sin, and deviations into errors in life and doctrine.

If we could see how this Lord Jesus has been tried by His people since the beginning, we would be amazed at His patience and gentle dealings with them. It is said, indeed, "The Lord is very compassionate, slow to anger, and of great mercy." If He had not been so, He could never have endured their behavior from Adam until now. Therefore, His compassion and mercy towards His church are preferred above a mother's compassion for her child. "Can a woman forget her nursing child, and not have compassion on the son of her womb? Yes, they may forget, yet I will not forget you," says the Lord (Isaiah 49:15).

God once gave Moses, as Christ's servant, a handful of His people to carry in his bosom, but only from Egypt to Canaan. Moses, as the Holy Spirit describes him, was the meekest man on earth; he loved the people greatly. Yet, neither his meekness nor love could sustain him in this task. He failed and became passionate, provoking his God to anger during this work. "And Moses said to the Lord, 'Why have You afflicted Your servant?'" But what was the affliction? The Lord had said to him, "Carry this people in your bosom as a nursing father bears the suckling child, to the land which You swore to their fathers."

Moses responded, "I am not able to bear all this people alone, because it is too heavy for me. If You deal with me this way, kill me, I pray, out of hand, and let me not see my wretchedness" (Numbers 11:11-15).

God gave them to Moses so that he might carry them in his bosom and show gentleness and patience towards them under all the provocations they would present from that time until he brought them to their land. However, he failed in this task; he could not exercise it because he lacked sufficient patience.

Now, it is said of the person speaking in the text, "He shall gather the lambs with His arm, and carry them in His bosom, and shall gently lead those that are with young" (Isaiah 40:11). This indicates that this was one of the qualifications God sought and knew was present in Him when He gave His elect to Him to save them.

4. The Father's giving them to Him to save them declares that He

possesses sufficient wisdom to handle all the difficulties that would arise in bringing His sons and daughters to glory. He has been made wisdom for us; indeed, He is called wisdom itself (1 Corinthians 1:30). Moreover, God says that "He shall deal prudently" (Isaiah 52:13).

The one who takes on the role of Savior must be wise, as their adversaries are exceedingly subtle. They must confront the serpent, who outwitted our first parents when their wisdom was at its peak (Genesis 3). But when it comes to wisdom, our Jesus is wise—wiser than Solomon, wiser than all men, wiser than all angels; He is indeed the wisdom of God. "Christ is the wisdom of God" (1 Corinthians 1:24). Hence, He turns sin, temptations, persecutions, falls, and all things to good for His people (Romans 8:28).

Now, these conclusions demonstrate the great and wonderful love of the Father in choosing one so well-prepared for the work of man's salvation.

Herein, indeed, we perceive the love of God. Huram gathered that God loved Israel because He had given them such a king as Solomon (2 Chronicles 2:11). But how much more can we behold the love that God has bestowed upon us, in that He has given us to His Son, and also given His Son for us?

5. The Son: Receiver of the Gift

"All that the Father gives Me shall come." In these words, there is a clear answer to the Father's purpose in giving His elect to Jesus Christ. The Father's intention was that they might come to Him and be saved by Him. The Son affirms that this will indeed happen; neither sin nor Satan, neither flesh nor the world, neither wisdom nor folly shall hinder their coming to Him. "They shall come to Me; and him who comes to Me I will in no wise cast out."

Here, therefore, the Lord Jesus decisively determines to provide a sufficient measure of grace that will effectively fulfill this promise. "They shall come;" that is, He will cause them to come by infusing an effective blessing into all the means that will be used for that purpose.

As it was said to the evil spirit sent to persuade Ahab to go and fall at Ramoth-Gilead, "Go: you shall persuade him, and prevail also: go forth, and do so" (1 Kings 22:22). In the same way, Jesus Christ will command the means used to bring those to Him whom the Father has given Him. He will bless those means effectively for this very end; they shall persuade them and prevail as well. Otherwise, as I mentioned, the Father's purpose would be thwarted.

The Father's will is that "of all which He has given Him, He should lose nothing, but should raise it up at the last day" (John 6:39). This is in order of priority: first Christ, the firstfruits, and afterward those who are His at His coming (1 Corinthians 15). However, this cannot be accomplished unless there is a work of grace effectively wrought in each one of them. But this work shall not fail to be accomplished in all whom the Father has given Him to save. "All that the Father has given Me shall come to Me," and so forth.

But to speak more clearly about the words, "They shall come," I would like to show you two things from these words – First, what it is to come to Christ. Second, what force there is in this promise to make them come to Him.

6. What It Means to Come to Christ

First, I would like to explain what it is to come to Christ. This term "come" must be understood spiritually, not carnally. Many came to Him in a physical sense, without any saving benefit from Him. Multitudes approached Him during His earthly ministry; indeed, countless crowds did so.

There is also, even today, a formal and customary coming to His ordinances and ways of worship, which is of no value. However, I will not address that now, as it is not the focus of this text.

The coming intended in the text refers to the movement of the mind towards Him, specifically the inclination of the heart towards Him. This movement arises from a genuine awareness of the absolute need that a person has for Him for justification and salvation.

This description of coming to Christ can be divided into two parts:

1. Coming to Christ is a movement of the mind towards Him.

2. This movement of the mind towards Him arises from a genuine awareness of the absolute need that a person has for Him for justification and salvation.

To address the first point, that it is a movement of the mind towards Him, this is evident; because coming here or there, if it is voluntary, is an act of the mind or will. Thus, coming to Christ is through the inclination of the will. "Your people shall be willing" (Psalm 110:3). This willingness of heart is what sets the mind in motion towards Him.

The church expresses this movement of her mind towards Christ by the movement of her affections. "My beloved put in His hand by the hole of the door, and my bowels were moved for Him" (Song of Solomon 5:4). "My bowels;" refers to the passions of my mind and affections, which are expressed by the yearning and stirring of the bowels, the passionate working of them, or their making a noise for Him (Genesis 43:30; 1 Kings 3:26; Isaiah 16:11).

This, then, is the coming to Christ: a movement towards Him with the mind. "And it shall come to pass that everything that lives, which moves, wherever the rivers shall come, shall live" (Ezekiel 47:9). The water in this text represents the grace of God in the doctrine of it. The living things are the children of men, to whom the grace of God, by the gospel, is preached. Now, He says, every living thing which moves, wherever the water shall come, shall live.

Moreover, see how this word "moves" is explained by Christ Himself in the book of Revelation: "The Spirit and the bride say, 'Come.' And let him who hears say, 'Come.' And let him who is thirsty come. And whoever will, let him take the water of life freely" (Revelation 22:17).

Thus, to move in your mind and will towards Christ is to be coming to Him. There are many poor souls who are coming to Christ but cannot articulate how to believe it, because they think that coming to Him is some strange and wonderful thing; and indeed, it is. However, they overlook the inclination of their will, the movement of their mind, and the stirring of their affections after Him; and they consider these as none of this strange and wonderful thing. When, in fact, it is one of the greatest wonders in this world to see a person who was once dead in sin, possessed by the devil, an enemy to Christ and to all things spiritually good, now moving with his mind towards the Lord Jesus Christ. This is one of the highest wonders in the world.

Second, it is a movement of the mind towards Him, stemming from a sound sense of the absolute need that a person has of Him for justification and salvation. Indeed, without this sense of a lost condition without Him, there will be no movement of the mind towards Him. There may be a movement of their mouths; "With their mouths they show much love" (Ezekiel 33:31). Such a people may come as the true people come; that is, in show and outward appearance. They may sit before God's ministers as His people sit before them; and they may hear His words too, but they will not do them; that is, they will not come inwardly with their minds. "For with their mouths they show much love, but their hearts," or minds, "go after their covetousness."

All this is because they lack an effective sense of the misery of their state by nature; for not until they have that will they, in their minds, move towards Him. Therefore, it is said concerning the true comers, "At that day the great trumpet shall be blown, and they shall come who were ready to perish in the land of Assyria, and the outcasts in the land of Egypt, and shall worship the Lord in the holy mount at Jerusalem" (Isaiah 27:13). They are, as you see, the outcasts and those who are ready to perish, who indeed have their minds effectively moved to come to Jesus Christ. This sense of things was what made the three thousand come, what made Saul come, what made the jailer come, and what indeed makes all others come who come effectively (Acts 2:8, 18).

The true coming to Christ is famously illustrated by the four lepers, as described in 2 Kings 7:3. During a severe famine in the land, there was no food for the people. The only sustenance available was the flesh of donkeys and the dung of doves, which was found only in Samaria. The lepers, however, had no access to this food because they were cast out of the city.

As they sat at the city gate, hunger was consuming them. Being half dead already, they began to consider their options. They expressed their dire situation to one another, saying, "If we enter the city, we will die from the famine there; if we stay here, we will die as well. Therefore, let us go to the camp of the Syrians. If they spare us, we will live; if they kill us, we will die."

Here, necessity drove them to seek life where they otherwise would not have gone. This mirrors the experience of those who truly come to Jesus Christ. They recognize death looming before them; they feel its grip, and they understand that it will consume them if they do not turn to Christ. Thus, they come out of necessity, compelled by the realization that they are utterly and eternally lost without Him. These are the ones who will come, and indeed, these are the ones who are invited to come: "Come to Me, all you who labor and are heavy laden, and I will give you rest" (Matthew 11:28).

To clarify further, coming to Christ arises from a genuine awareness of the absolute need that a person has for Him, as previously mentioned.

"They shall come with weeping, and with supplications will I lead them; I will cause them to walk by the rivers of waters in a straight way wherein they shall not stumble" (Jeremiah 31:9). Notice that they come with weeping and supplication; they approach with prayers and tears. These expressions are the results of a true understanding of their need for mercy. A person who is insensitive to their condition cannot come; they cannot pray or cry out because they do not perceive or feel their need.

"In those days, and at that time, the children of Israel shall come; they and the children of Judah together, going and weeping. They shall go and seek the Lord their God. They shall ask the way to Zion with their faces toward it, saying, 'Come, and let us join ourselves to the Lord in a perpetual covenant that shall not be forgotten'" (Jeremiah 50:4-5).

Coming to Christ is described as running to Him, as fleeing from impending wrath. This language conveys the urgency felt by the person coming to Him; they are acutely aware of their sin and the death that it brings. They understand that the avenger of blood is pursuing them, and thus they must hasten to the Son of God for life (Matthew 3:7; Psalm 143:9).

Fleeing is the last resort for someone in danger. Not everyone who recognizes danger will flee; many will first consider other means of escape. Therefore, fleeing is the final action taken when all other options have failed. When a person realizes that their only alternatives are sin, death, and damnation unless they run to Christ for life, then they will flee, but not until that moment.

The true coming to Christ stems from a deep sense of absolute need for His salvation. This is evident in the cries of those who come to Him, such as "Lord, save me, or I perish!" and "Men and brethren, what shall we do?" or "Sirs, what must I do to be saved?" (Matthew 14:30; Acts 2:37; 16:30).

This language clearly reveals that those who truly come are aware of their need for salvation through Jesus Christ and recognize that no one else can help them but Him.

This understanding is further illustrated by the fact that such individuals are "pricked in their heart," meaning they feel the weight of the death sentence imposed by the law. Even a slight prick in the heart can be fatal (Acts 2:37). They are described as weeping, trembling, and being astonished at the evident and unavoidable danger they face unless they flee to Jesus Christ (Acts 9:16).

Coming to Christ is accompanied by a genuine and sincere forsaking of all else for Him. "If anyone comes to Me and does not hate his father and mother, wife and children, brothers and sisters, yes, and his own life also, he cannot be My disciple. And whoever does not bear his cross and come after Me cannot be My disciple" (Luke 14:26-27).

Through these and similar expressions, Christ describes the true seeker, the one who is genuinely coming to Him. This person casts aside everything that might hinder their approach to Jesus Christ.

There are many who pretend to come to Christ, much like the man in Matthew 21:30, who said to his father, "I go, Sir," but did not go. Many such pretenders respond to Christ's call through the gospel, saying, "I come, Sir," yet they remain attached to their pleasures and worldly desires. They do not truly come; they merely offer a polite compliment. Christ takes note of this and will not regard it as anything more than a lie.

He said, "I go, Sir, and went not;" he deceived himself and lied. Beware of this, you who flatter yourselves with your own deceptions. Words alone will not suffice with Jesus Christ. Coming means coming, and nothing else will suffice.

Before addressing the next topic, I will respond to some objections that often arise for those who are genuinely seeking to come to Jesus Christ.

Objection: Although I cannot deny that my mind is drawn to Christ, motivated by a recognition of my lost condition, knowing that without Him I perish, I fear that my intentions in coming to Him are not right.

Question: What is your purpose in coming to Christ?

Answer: My purpose is to receive life and to be saved by Jesus Christ.

Let me clarify that coming to Christ for life and salvation, even if that is your only intention at the moment, is a legitimate and commendable approach to Jesus Christ.

This is evident because Christ presents life as the primary reason for sinners to come to Him. He also criticizes them for not coming to Him for life, as seen in His words, "And you will not come to Me, that you might have life" (John 5:40).

Moreover, there are many other Scriptures where He invites sinners to come to Him, emphasizing their safety. For instance, "whoever believes in Him should not perish;" "he who believes has passed from death unto life;" "he who believes will be saved;" and "he who believes in Him is not condemned."

Believing and coming are essentially the same act. Thus, it is clear that coming to Christ for life is a valid and good approach. By believing that He alone has made atonement for sin (Romans 2), you honor Him greatly.

He honors the word of Christ and agrees with its truth in two main ways:

1. He agrees with the truth of all those statements that declare sin to be utterly abominable in itself, dishonorable to God, and damning to the soul of man; for this is the testimony of the one who comes to Jesus Christ (Jeremiah 44:4; Romans 2:23; 6:23; 2 Thessalonians 2:12).

2. He believes, as the word states, that in the best things of the world, including righteousness, there is nothing but death and damnation; for this too is the belief of the one who comes to Jesus Christ for life (Romans 7:24-25; 8:2-3; 2 Corinthians 3:6-8).

He honors Christ's person by believing that there is life in Him and that He is capable of saving him from death, hell, the devil, and damnation; for unless a person believes this, they will not come to Christ for life (Hebrews 7:24-25).

He honors Him by believing that He is authorized by the Father to grant life to those who come to Him for it (John 5:11-12; 17:1-3).

He honors the priesthood of Jesus Christ in two ways:

1. By believing that Christ has more power to save from sin through the sacrifice He has offered than all laws, devils, death, or sin have to condemn. Anyone who does not believe this will not come to Jesus Christ for life (Acts 13:38; Hebrews 2:14-15; Revelation 1:17-18).

2. By believing that Christ, in accordance with His office, will be most faithful and merciful in fulfilling His role. This belief must be included in the faith of anyone who comes to Jesus Christ for life (1 John 2:1-3; Hebrews 2:17-18).

Furthermore, the one who comes to Jesus Christ for life takes a stand with Him against sin and against the flawed and imperfect righteousness of the world; indeed, they stand against false Christs and damnable errors that oppose the worthiness of His merits and sufficiency. This is evident because such a soul chooses Christ above all others as the only one who can save.

Therefore, just as Noah prepared the ark at God's command for his own salvation, by which he also condemned the world and became an heir of the righteousness that is by faith (Hebrews 11:7), so too, coming sinner, be assured; the one who comes to Jesus Christ also believes that He is willing to show mercy and have compassion upon him, even though he is unworthy. Thus, your soul is not only under a special invitation to come but also under a promise of acceptance and forgiveness (Matthew 11:28).

All these specific aspects and qualities of faith are present in the soul that comes to Jesus Christ for life, as is evident to any fair judgment. For will someone who does not believe the testimony of Christ regarding the wretchedness of sin and the inadequacy of worldly righteousness come to Christ for life? No. The one who does not believe this testimony does not come. The one who believes that life can be found elsewhere does not come. The one who questions whether the Father has given Christ the authority to forgive does not come. The one who thinks that sin, the law, death, and the devil pose a greater threat than Christ can save does not come. Likewise, anyone who doubts His faithful management of His priesthood for the salvation of sinners does not come.

You, then, who are indeed the coming sinner, believe all of this. It may be true that you do not believe with complete assurance, nor do you have the time to notice your faith in these distinct acts; yet, all of this faith is present in you as you come to Christ for life. The faith that works in this way is of the best and purest kind because this person comes solely as a sinner, recognizing that life is found only in Jesus Christ.

Before I conclude my response to this objection, consider these two things.

1. Consider that the cities of refuge were established for those who were dead in the law but sought to live by grace. They were for those who fled there for life from the avenger of blood pursuing them. It is worth noting that those who were on their way to these cities are specifically called the people of God: "Cast up, cast up," says God; "prepare the way; take the stumbling block out of the way of my people" (Isaiah 57:14). This refers to preparing the way to the city of refuge so that the slayers might escape there; these fleeing slayers are, in a special way, called the people of God, even those who escaped there for life.

2. Consider the case of Ahab when Benhadad sent to him for life, saying, "Thus says your servant Benhadad, I pray you, let me live." Although Benhadad had sought Ahab's crown, kingdom, and even his life, how effectively did Benhadad prevail with him! Ahab asked, "Is Benhadad still alive?" He said, "He is my brother." So, he commanded, "Go, bring him to me." Thus, he made him ride in his chariot (1 Kings 20).

Coming sinner, what do you think? If Jesus Christ had as little goodness in Him as Ahab, He might grant a humble Benhadad life; you are not asking for His crown and dignity; eternal life will suffice for you. How much more, then, will you receive it since you are dealing with Him who is goodness and mercy itself! Moreover, you are called upon and greatly encouraged by a promise of life to come to Him for life! Read also these Scriptures: Numbers 35:11, 14, 15; Joshua 20:1-6; Hebrews 6:16-21.

Objection. When I say I only seek myself, I mean that I do not find that I am aiming for God's glory in my own salvation through Christ, and this makes me fear that I do not come rightly.

Answer. Where does Christ Jesus require such a qualification from those who are coming to Him for life? Come to Him for life, and do not trouble yourself with such objections against yourself. Let God and Christ glorify themselves in the salvation of such a worm as you are.

The Father says to the Son, "You are my servant, O Israel, in whom I will be glorified." God offers life to sinners as the reason to persuade them to come to Him for life; and Christ plainly says, "I have come that they may have life" (John 10:10). He has no need of your designs, though you have need of His. Eternal life, pardon of sin, and deliverance from wrath to come are what Christ offers to you, and these are the things you need. Besides, God will be gracious and merciful to worthless, undeserving wretches; therefore, come as such a one, and do not lay any stumbling blocks in the way to Him, but come to Him for life and live (John 5:34; 10:10; 3:36; Matthew 1:21; Proverbs 8:35-36; 1 Thessalonians 1:10; John 11:25-26).

When the jailer asked, "Sirs, what must I do to be saved?" Paul did not once ask him, "What is your intention in this question? Are you seeking the glory of God in the salvation of your soul?" He had more wisdom; he understood that such questions would only lead to foolish babble instead of providing a sufficient answer.

Seeing this poor wretch lacked salvation through Jesus Christ, meaning he wanted to be saved from hell and death, which he knew was due to him for the sins he had committed, Paul instructed him, as a condemned sinner, to continue in his pursuit of self-seeking. He said, "Believe on the Lord Jesus Christ, and you shall be saved" (Acts 16:30-32).

I know that later you will desire to glorify Christ by walking in the way of His precepts, but for now, you need life. The avenger of blood is behind you, and the devil is like a roaring lion pursuing you. So, come now and obtain life from these threats. Once you have received a comforting assurance that you are a partaker of life through Christ, then, and not until then, will you say, "Bless the Lord, O my soul, and all that is within me bless His holy name. Bless the Lord, O my soul, and forget not all His benefits: who forgives all your iniquities, who heals all your diseases; who redeems your life from destruction; who crowns you with lovingkindness and tender mercies" (Psalm 103:1-4).

Objection. But I cannot believe that I come to Christ rightly because sometimes I am prone to question His very existence and His office to save.

To do so is horrible; but could you not be judging incorrectly in this matter? How can I judge incorrectly when I judge based on how I feel? Poor soul! You may judge incorrectly despite that. You say, "I think these questions arise from my heart." Let me respond. What comes from your heart comes from your will and affections, from your understanding, judgment, and conscience, for these must agree with your questioning if your questioning is heartfelt. And how do you say, for example, do you with your affections and conscience question this? Answer: No, my conscience trembles when such thoughts enter my mind, and my affections are inclined otherwise.

Then I conclude that these thoughts are either suddenly injected by the devil, or they are the fruits of the body of sin and death that still dwells within you, or perhaps they come from both sources together.

If these thoughts come entirely from the devil, as they seem to, because your conscience and affections are against them, or if they arise from that body of death within you, do not be overly concerned about their origin. The safest approach is to take responsibility for your own actions. None of this should hinder your coming to Christ, nor should it lead you to conclude that you are not approaching Him correctly. Before I conclude, let me ask you a few questions about this matter.

Do you like these wicked blasphemies?

Answer: No, no, their presence and influence kill me.

Do you mourn for them, pray against them, and hate yourself because of them?

Answer: Yes, yes; but what troubles me is that I do not prevail against them.

If you could choose, would you sincerely want your heart to be affected and taken with the things that are best, most heavenly, and holy?

Answer: With all my heart, I would choose death the next hour, if it were God's will, rather than to sin against Him in this way.

Well then, your dislike of these thoughts, your mourning over them, your prayers against them, and your self-loathing because of them, along with your sincere desire for thoughts that are heavenly and holy, clearly indicate that these thoughts do not align with your will, affections, understanding, judgment, or conscience.

Therefore, your heart is not in them. Rather, they come directly from the devil or arise from the body of death that is within you. You should say, "Now, then, it is no longer I who do it, but sin that dwells in me" (Romans 7:17).

I will give you a relevant example. In Deuteronomy 22, you can read about a betrothed young woman, one who is engaged to her beloved, having given him her heart and voice, just as you have given yourself to Christ. Yet, she was encountered while walking in the field by a man who forced her, because he was stronger than she. What judgment does God, the righteous judge, pass upon the young woman for this? "The man who lay with her," says God, "shall die. But to the young woman, you shall do nothing; there is no sin in the young woman worthy of death. For, as when a man rises against his neighbor and kills him, so is this matter; for he found her in the field, and the betrothed young woman cried out, and there was no one to save her" (Deuteronomy 22:25-27).

You are this young woman. The man who forced you with these blasphemous thoughts is the devil; he comes upon you at a vulnerable moment, even while you are wandering after Jesus Christ. But you cry out, and by your cry, you show that you abhor such wickedness. The Judge of all the earth will do what is right; He will not hold the sin against you, but against the one who offered the violence. For your comfort, consider this: He came to heal those "who were oppressed by the devil" (Acts 10:38).

Objection. But, says another, I am so heartless, so slow, and, as I think, so indifferent in my coming, that, to be honest, I do not know whether my kind of coming should even be called a coming to Christ.

Answer. You know that I told you from the beginning that coming to Christ is a movement of the heart and affections toward Him.

But, says the soul, my dullness and indifference in all holy duties demonstrate my heartlessness in coming. To come without the heart signifies nothing at all.

The movement of the heart toward Christ is not always discerned by your outward performance of duties. Instead, it is often revealed through the secret groanings and complaints your soul makes to God against the sloth that accompanies you in those duties.

But even if you say that you come slowly, since Christ invites those who do not come at all, surely He will accept those who do come, even if they are burdened with the infirmities you currently struggle with. He says, "and him that comes to Me I will in no wise cast out." He does not say, "If they come quickly or with great feeling," but rather, "and him that comes to Me I will in no wise cast out." He also says in Proverbs 9, "As for him who lacks understanding," meaning a heart (for often understanding is equated with the heart), "come, eat of my bread, and drink of the wine which I have mingled."

You may be fervent in spirit when coming to Jesus Christ, yet still struggle with feelings of sloth. This was true of the church when she cried, "Draw me, we will run after You." It was also true for Paul when he said, "When I would do good, evil is present with me" (Song of Solomon 1:4; Romans 7; Galatians 5:19). The works, struggles, and oppositions of the flesh are more evident than the works of the Spirit in our hearts, and they are felt more readily. So, what should we do? Let us not be discouraged by the sight and feeling of our own infirmities, but rather run faster to Jesus Christ for salvation.

Warm your heart with the sweet promise of Christ's acceptance of the coming sinner, and that will encourage you to hasten toward Him. Discouraging thoughts are like cold weather; they numb the senses and make us clumsy in our endeavors. However, the sweet and warm rays of promise are like the comforting beams of the sun, which invigorate and refresh. You can see how little the bee and fly are active in the air during winter; the cold hinders them. But when the wind and sun are warm, who is busier than they?

But again, he who comes to Christ is fleeing for his life. No one who is fleeing for their life thinks they are moving quickly enough on their journey; if they could, they would gladly take a mile in a single step. "Oh, my sloth and heartlessness!" you say. "Oh, that I had wings like a dove! For then I would fly away and be at rest. I would hasten my escape from the windy storm and tempest" (Psalm 55:6, 8).

Poor coming soul, you are like a man who wishes to ride at full gallop, but whose horse can barely trot! The desire of his heart should not be judged by the slow pace of the dull horse he rides, but by the fidgeting, kicking, and spurring he does while sitting on its back. Your flesh is like this dull horse; it will not gallop after Christ. It will lag behind, even though your soul and eternal life are at stake. But take comfort; Christ does not judge according to the intensity of outward motion (Mark 10:17) but according to the sincerity of the heart and the inner person (John 1:47; Psalm 51:6; Matthew 26:41).

Ziba, in appearance, came to David much faster than Mephibosheth did; yet his heart was not as upright toward David as Mephibosheth's. It is true that Mephibosheth received a rebuke from David, who asked, "Why did you not go with me, Mephibosheth?" However, when David remembered that Mephibosheth was lame—his plea being, "Your servant is lame" (2 Samuel 19)—he was content and concluded that

Mephibosheth would have come after him faster if he could. Mephibosheth appealed to David, who was like an angel of God during those days, knowing all things done on earth, to confirm that the reason for his slowness lay in his lameness, not in his will.

Poor coming sinner, you may not be able to come to Christ with the outward swiftness of a courier like many others do. But does the reason for your slowness lie in your mind and will, or in the sluggishness of the flesh? Can you sincerely say, "The spirit indeed is willing, but the flesh is weak" (Matthew 26:41)? Can you appeal to the Lord Jesus, who knows the innermost thoughts of your heart, that this is true? Then take this as your comfort: He has said, "I will assemble her that halts; I will make her that halted a remnant" (Micah 4:6), "and I will save her that halts" (Zephaniah 3:19). What more could you desire from the sweet lips of the Son of God?

I also read of some who are to follow Christ in chains; I say, to come after Him in chains. "Thus says the Lord: The labor of Egypt, and the merchandise of Ethiopia and of the Sabeans, men of stature, shall come over to you, and they shall be yours. They shall come after you in chains, and they shall fall down to you, making supplication to you, saying, 'Surely there is no other to save'" (Isaiah 45:14). Surely those who come after Christ in chains do so with great difficulty, as their steps are constrained by the chains. And what chains are heavier than those that discourage you? Your chain, made up of guilt and filth, is heavy; it is a wretched bond around your neck, causing your strength to fail (Lamentations 1:14; 3:18). But come, even if you come in chains; it is a glory to Christ that a sinner comes after Him in chains. The clinking of your chains, though troublesome to you, cannot obstruct your salvation. It is Christ's work and glory to save you from your chains, to enlarge your steps, and to set you free. The blind man, though called, could not quickly come to Jesus Christ, but Christ could stand still and wait for him (Mark 10:49). True, "He rides upon the wings of the wind," yet He is long-suffering, and His long-suffering is salvation for those who come to Him (2 Peter 3:9).

If you had seen those who came to the Lord Jesus during His earthly ministry, how slowly and haltingly they approached Him due to their infirmities, and how kindly and graciously He received them, granting them the desires of their hearts, you would not make such objections against yourself in your coming to Jesus Christ as you do now.

Object. But, says another, I fear I come too late. I doubt I have stayed too long. I am afraid the door is shut.

Answer. You can never come too late to Jesus Christ if you truly come.

This is evident through two examples.

The first example is the man who came to him at the eleventh hour. This man was idle all day long. He had the entire day to come in, yet he wasted it all except for the last hour. However, at the eleventh hour, he finally came and entered the vineyard to work alongside the other laborers who had borne the burden and heat of the day.

How was he received by the lord of the vineyard? When payday arrived, he received the same amount as the others; in fact, he was paid first. It is true that the others complained about this, but what did the Lord Jesus say in response? "Is your eye evil because I am good? I will give to this last man the same as I give to you" (Matthew 20:14-15).

The second example is the thief on the cross. He also came late, just an hour before his death. He had stayed away from Jesus Christ for as long as he could while living as a thief, and even longer. If he could have deceived the judge and escaped his rightful punishment through lies, he might not have come to his Savior at all. However, being convicted and condemned to die, fastened to the cross, he found himself in a desperate situation.

At that moment, when this wicked man sought mercy from Jesus, the Lord responded to him without any mention of his past misdeeds, saying, "Today you will be with me in paradise" (Luke 23:43). Let no one misuse this grace of God for their own indulgence. My purpose now is to encourage the coming soul.

Object. But is the door of mercy not shut against some before they die?

Answer. Yes, and God forbids that prayers should be made for them (Jeremiah 6:16; Jude 22).

Question. Then, why should I not doubt that I may be one of those?

Answer. By no means, if you are coming to Jesus Christ. When God shuts the door on people, He does not give them a heart to come to Jesus Christ. "No one comes unless it has been given to him by the Father." But you are coming, therefore it has been given to you by the Father.

Be assured, therefore, that if the Father has given you a heart to come to Jesus Christ, the gate of mercy still stands open to you. It is not in accordance with the wisdom of God to give you the strength to come to birth and then shut the womb (Isaiah 66:9); to grant you grace to come to Jesus Christ and then close the door of His mercy against you. "Incline your ear," He says, "and come to Me; hear, and your soul shall live; and I will make an everlasting covenant with you, even the sure mercies of David" (Isaiah 55:3).

Object. But it is said that some knocked when the door was shut.

Answer. Yes, but the texts that mention those who knock refer to the day of judgment, not to the sinner coming to Christ in this life. See the texts, Matthew 15:11, Luke 13:24, 25. Therefore, these do not concern you at all, since you are coming to Jesus Christ; you are coming NOW! "Now is the accepted time; behold, now is the day of salvation" (2 Corinthians 6:2).

Now God is upon the mercy seat; now Christ Jesus sits beside Him, continually pleading the victory of His blood for sinners. As long as this world lasts, this word of the text shall still be free and fully fulfilled: "And him that comes to Me I will in no wise cast out."

Sinner, the greater sinner you are, the greater your need for mercy, and the more Christ will be glorified through it. Come then, come and try; come, taste and see how good the Lord is to an undeserving sinner!

Object. But, says another, I have fallen since I began to come to Christ; therefore I fear I did not come correctly, and consequently that Christ will not receive me.

Answer. Falls are dangerous because they dishonor Christ, wound the conscience, and cause the enemies of God to speak reproachfully. However, it is not a valid argument to say, "I have fallen, therefore I was not coming correctly to Jesus Christ." If David, Solomon, and Peter had objected in this way, they would have only added to their grief; yet they had at least as much cause as you do.

A person whose steps are ordered by the Lord, and whose goings the Lord delights in, may still be overtaken by a temptation that causes them to fall (Psalm 37:23, 24). Did not Aaron fall? Yes, and Moses himself? What shall we say of Hezekiah and Jehoshaphat?

There are, therefore, different kinds of falls; some are pardonable, and some are unpardonable. Unpardonable falls are those against light, from the faith, leading to the despising and trampling upon Jesus Christ and His blessed undertakings (Hebrews 6:2-5; 10:28, 29). For such individuals, there remains no more sacrifice for sin. Indeed, they have no heart, no mind, and no desire to come to Jesus Christ for life; therefore, they must perish.

Nay, says the Holy Spirit, "It is impossible that they should be renewed again unto repentance." Therefore, God has no compassion for them, nor should we; but for other falls, though they may be dreadful, and God will chastise His people for them, they do not prove you to be a graceless person, one who is not coming to Jesus Christ for life.

It is said of the child in the gospel that while "he was yet coming, the devil threw him down and tore him" (Luke 9:42). Dejected sinner, it is no wonder that you have stumbled while coming to Jesus Christ. Is it not rather surprising that you have not stumbled a thousand times before this? Consider:

1. What fools we are by nature.

2. What weaknesses are in us.

3. What mighty powers the fallen angels, our implacable enemies, possess.

4. How often the one who is coming is benighted in his journey, and what stumbling blocks lie in their way.

5. How their familiar companions, who were so before, now watch for their halting and seek to cause them to fall by the hand of their strong ones.

What then? Must we, because of these temptations, incline to fall? No. Must we not fear falls? Yes. "Let him who thinks he stands take heed lest he fall" (1 Corinthians 10:12). Yet let him not be utterly cast down; "The Lord upholds all who fall and raises up those who are bowed down."

Do not make light of falls! Yet, if you have fallen, "You have," said Samuel, "done all this wickedness; yet turn not aside from following the Lord," but serve Him with a perfect heart, and turn not aside, "for the Lord will not forsake His people," and He counts the coming sinner as one of them, "because it has pleased the Lord to make you His people" (1 Samuel 12:20-22).

7. The Promise's Power to Draw People to Christ

"Shall come to Me." Now we come to show what force there is in this promise to make them come to Him. "All that the Father gives Me shall come to Me." I will speak to this promise, first, in general, and second, in particular.

First, in general. This word "shall" is confined to all who are given to Christ. "All that the Father gives Me shall come to Me." Hence, I conclude that coming to Jesus Christ rightly is an effect of their being given to Christ by God beforehand.

Mark, they shall come. Who? Those that are given. They come because they were given: "Thine they were, and Thou gavest them Me." Now, this is indeed a singular comfort to those who are coming in truth to Christ, to think that the reason why they come is that they were given by the Father to Him beforehand.

Thus, the coming soul may reason with themselves as they come: Am I truly coming to Jesus Christ? This coming of mine is not to be attributed to me or my goodness, but to the grace and gift of God to Christ. God first gave my person to Him, and therefore has now given me a heart to come.

This word "shall come" makes your coming not only the fruit of the gift of the Father but also of the purpose of the Son; for these words express a Divine purpose. They show us the heavenly determination of the Son: "The Father has given them to Me, and they shall; yes, they shall come to Me."

Christ is as resolute in His determination to save those given to Him as the Father is in giving them. Christ values the gift of His Father; He will lose nothing of it. He is resolved to save it entirely by His blood and to raise it up again at the last day; thus, He fulfills His Father's will and accomplishes His own desires (John 6:39).

These words "shall come" also make your coming the effect of an absolute promise. Coming sinner, you are included in a promise; your coming is the fruit of the faithfulness of an absolute promise. It was this promise, by the virtue of which you first received the strength to come.

And this is the promise, by virtue of which you shall be effectively brought to Him. It was said to Abraham, "At this time I will come, and Sarah shall have a son." This son was Isaac. Notice! "Sarah shall have a son;" there is the promise. And Sarah had a son; there was the fulfillment of the promise; and therefore, Isaac was called the child of the promise (Genesis 17:19; 18:10; Romans 9:9).

"Sarah shall have a son." But how, if Sarah is past the age? Still, the promise continues to say, "Sarah shall have a son." But how, if Sarah is barren? The promise still says, "Sarah shall have a son." But Abraham's body is now dead? The promise remains the same: "Sarah shall have a son."

Thus, you see what power there is in an absolute promise; it carries enough within itself to accomplish the thing promised, whether there are means or not in us to effect it. Therefore, this promise in the text, being an absolute promise, means that by virtue of it—not by virtue of ourselves or our own efforts—we come to Jesus Christ. For so are the words of the text: "All that the Father gives Me shall come to Me."

Therefore, every sincere person who comes to Jesus Christ is also called a child of the promise. "Now we, brethren, as Isaac was, are children of promise" (Galatians 4:28); that is, we are the children that God has promised to Jesus Christ and given to Him. Yes, the children that Jesus Christ has promised shall come to Him. "All that the Father gives Me shall come."

This word "shall come" engages Christ to communicate all kinds of grace to those given to Him, to make them effectively come to Him. "They shall come;" that is, not if they will, but if grace, all grace, if power, wisdom, a new heart, and the Holy Spirit—all joining together—can make them come.

I say, this word "shall come," being absolute, has no dependence on our own will, power, or goodness; but it engages for us even God Himself, Christ Himself, the Spirit Himself. When God made that absolute promise to Abraham that Sarah "should have a son," Abraham did not look for any qualification in himself because the promise looked at none.

As God had, by the promise, absolutely promised him a son, he did not consider his own body, now dead, nor the barrenness of Sarah's womb. "He did not waver at the promise of God through unbelief, but was strengthened in faith, giving glory to God, and being fully convinced that what He had promised He was also able to perform" (Romans 4:20-21).

He had promised, and had promised absolutely, "Sarah shall have a son." Therefore, Abraham expected that God must fulfill the condition of it. This expectation of Abraham is not disapproved by the Holy Spirit but is considered good and commendable, as it was by this that he gave glory to God.

The Father has also given to Christ a certain number of souls for Him to save; and He Himself has said, "They shall come to Him." Let the church of God then live in joyful expectation of the complete fulfillment of this promise; for assuredly it shall be fulfilled, and not even a tiny part of it shall fail. "They SHALL come to Me."

And now, before I go any further, I will inquire more specifically into the nature of an absolute promise.

We call that an absolute promise which is made without any condition; or more fully: An absolute promise of God, or of Christ, is one that grants this or that person any saving, spiritual blessing, without requiring any condition to be fulfilled on our part to obtain it. This is such a promise we have in hand. Let the best Master of Arts on earth show me, if he can, any condition in this text that depends upon any qualification in us, which is not concluded by the same promise, and shall be accomplished by the Lord Jesus in us.

An absolute promise, therefore, is, as we say, without "if" or "and"; that is, it requires nothing of us for it to be accomplished. It does not say, "They shall, if they will"; but "They shall." It does not say, "They shall, if they use the means"; but "They shall."

You may argue that a will and the use of means are implied, though not expressed. But I respond, no, by no means; that is not a condition of this promise. If they are included in the promise at all, they are included as the fruit of the absolute promise, not as if it expects the qualification to arise from us. "Your people shall be willing in the day of Your power" (Psalm 110:3). That is another absolute promise.

But does that promise suppose a willingness in us as a condition for God making us willing? "They shall be willing, if they are willing"; or, "They shall be willing, if they will be willing." This is ridiculous; there is nothing of this supposed. The promise is absolute concerning us; all that it engages for its own accomplishment is the mighty power of Christ and His faithfulness to fulfill it.

The difference, therefore, between the absolute and conditional promise is this:

They differ in their terms. The absolute promises say, "I will, and you shall"; while the conditional ones say, "I will, if you will"; or, "Do this, and you shall live" (Jeremiah 4:1; 31:31-33; Ezekiel 18:30-32; 36:24-34; Hebrews 8:7-13; Matthew 19:21).

They differ in their way of communicating good things to people. The absolute promises communicate things freely, solely by grace; while the conditional ones require that there be a qualification in us that the promise calls for, or else it does not apply.

The absolute promises, therefore, engage God; the conditional promises engage us. I mean, they involve God alone and us alone.

Absolute promises must be fulfilled; conditional promises may or may not be fulfilled. The absolute promises must be fulfilled because of God's faithfulness, while the conditional promises may not be fulfilled due to the unfaithfulness of men.

Absolute promises, therefore, have within themselves the sufficiency to bring about their own fulfillment; the conditional promises do not possess this quality. The absolute promise is like a large, bountiful promise because it contains within itself a fullness of all the desired things for us. When the time for that promise arrives, it will provide us mortals with what will truly save us and make us capable of fulfilling the demands of the conditional promise.

Therefore, although there is a real and eternal difference between the conditional and absolute promises, there is also a blessed harmony between them in other respects, as can be seen in the following particulars. The conditional promise calls for repentance, while the absolute promise grants it (Acts 5:31). The conditional promise calls for faith, and the absolute promise provides it (Zephaniah 3:12; Romans 15:12). The conditional promise calls for a new heart, and the absolute promise gives it (Ezekiel 36:25-26). The conditional promise demands holy obedience, while the absolute promise provides it or causes it (Ezekiel 36:27).

As they harmoniously agree in this way, the conditional promise blesses the person who is endowed with its fruit by the absolute promise. For example, the absolute promise makes people upright, and then the conditional promise follows, saying, "Blessed are the undefiled in the way, who walk in the law of the Lord" (Psalm 119:1). The absolute promise gives this person the fear of the Lord, and then the conditional promise follows, saying, "Blessed is everyone that fears the Lord" (Psalm 128:1). The absolute promise grants faith, and then the conditional promise follows, saying, "Blessed is she who believed" (Zephaniah 3:12; Luke 1:45). The absolute promise brings free forgiveness of sins, and then the conditional promise states, "Blessed are those whose iniquities are forgiven, and whose sins are covered" (Romans 4:7). The absolute promise assures that God's elect shall endure to the end; then the conditional promise follows with its blessings, "He who endures to the end shall be saved" (1 Peter 1:4-6; Matthew 24:13).

Thus, the promises gloriously serve one another and us in this harmonious agreement.

Now, the promise under consideration is an absolute promise: "All that the Father gives Me shall come to Me."

This promise, therefore, is, as stated, a bountiful promise, containing within itself all those things that the conditional promises call for from us. They shall come! Will they come? Yes, they shall come. But how can they come if they lack those things—those graces, power, and heart—without which they cannot come? The phrase "shall come" addresses all these concerns and any other objections that may arise. Here, I will take the liberty to elaborate further.

Objections to the absoluteness of this promise (the force of "shall come") answered:

Objection. But they are dead, dead in trespasses and sins; how shall they then come?

Answer: The phrase "shall come" can raise them from this death. "The hour is coming, and now is, when the dead shall hear the voice of the Son of God, and those who hear shall live." Thus, this impediment is removed from the way by the phrase "shall come." They shall be healed; they shall live.

Objection. But they are captives of Satan; he takes them captive at his will, and he is stronger than they are. How then can they come?

Answer: The phrase "shall come" has also provided help for this.

Satan had bound that daughter of Abraham so that she could not lift herself up; yet "shall come" set her free both in body and soul. Christ will turn them from the power of Satan to God.

But must they turn themselves or do something to earn His favor in order to be turned? No, He will do it freely, of His own good will.

Alas! A person whose soul is possessed by the devil is turned wherever that governor wishes. They are taken captive by him, notwithstanding their natural powers, at his will. But what will he do? Will he hold them when "shall come" puts forth itself? Will he then let them come to Jesus Christ? No, that cannot be! His power is but the power of a fallen angel, but "shall come" is the Word of God. Therefore, "shall come" must be fulfilled; "and the gates of hell shall not prevail against it."

Mary Magdalene had seven devils, far too many for her to escape from their power. But when the time came for "shall come" to be fulfilled upon her, they gave way, fled from her, and she indeed came to Jesus Christ, as it is written, "All that the Father gives Me shall come to Me."

The man possessed with a legion (Mark 5) was too much captivated for him to come by human force. Even if he had all the men under heaven to help him, if the one who said, "He shall come" withheld His mighty power, he would not have been able to come.

But when this promise was to be fulfilled upon him, then he came; nor could all their power hinder his coming. It was also this "shall come" that preserved him from death when he was hurled hither and thither by these evil spirits. It was by the virtue of "shall come" that he was finally set at liberty from them and enabled to come to Christ. "All that the Father gives Me shall come to Me."

Objection. You say they shall come; but what if they will not? If that is the case, then what can "shall come" do?

Answer: True, there are some who say, "We are lords; we will come no more to You" (Jeremiah 2:31).

But as God says in another context, if they are involved in "shall come" to Me, they "shall know whose words will stand, Mine or theirs" (Jeremiah 41:28).

Here is the situation: we must now see who will be the liar — he who says, "I will not," or He who says, "He shall come to Me."

God says, "You shall come"; the sinner says, "I will not come." Now, as surely as he is involved in this "shall come," God will make that man eat his own words.

"I will not" is the unwise conclusion of a confused sinner, but "shall come" was spoken by Him who has the power to perform His word.

"Son, go work today in My vineyard," said the Father. But he answered, "I will not come." What now? Will he be able to stand by his refusal? Will he pursue his desperate denial? No, "he afterwards repented and went."

But how did he come by that repentance? It was wrapped up for him in the absolute promise; therefore, notwithstanding he said, "I will not," he afterwards repented and went.

By this parable, Jesus Christ illustrates the obstinacy of the sinners of the world regarding their coming to Him; they will not come, even when threatened, even when life is offered to them on the condition of coming.

But now, when "shall come," the absolute promise of God, is fulfilled upon them, then they come.

By that promise, a cure is provided against the rebellion of their will. "Your people shall be willing in the day of Your power" (Psalm 110:3).

Your people, what people? The people that Your Father has given You. The obstinacy and plague that is in the will of that people shall be taken away, and they shall be made willing. "Shall come" will make them willing to come to You.

He who had seen Paul in the midst of his outrages against Christ, His gospel, and His people, would hardly have thought that he would ever become a follower of Jesus Christ, especially since he did not act against his conscience in persecuting them.

He truly believed that he ought to do what he was doing. But we can see what "shall come" can do when it is fulfilled upon the soul of a rebellious sinner.

He was a chosen vessel, given by the Father to the Son; and now, when the time came for "shall come" to take him in hand, behold, he is overpowered, astonished, and trembling with reverence. In a moment, he becomes willing to be obedient to the heavenly call (Acts 9).

And were not those you read of (Acts 2) far gone, who had their hands and hearts in the murder of the Son of God? To show their determination never to repent of that horrid act, they said, "His blood be on us and on our children."

But must their obstinacy rule? Must they be bound to their own ruin by the rebellion of their stubborn wills? No, not those whom the Father gave to Christ.

Therefore, at the appointed times, "shall come" breaks in among them; the absolute promise takes them in hand; and then they indeed come, crying out to Peter and the rest of the apostles, "Men and brethren, what shall we do?"

No stubbornness of man's will can stand when God has absolutely said the contrary. "Shall come" can make them come "as doves to their windows," even those who had previously resolved never to come to Him.

The Lord spoke to Manasseh and to his people through the prophets, but would he listen? No, he would not.

But shall Manasseh escape this? No, he shall not. Therefore, being one of those whom the Father had given to the Son, and thus falling within the reach of "shall come," at last, "shall come" takes him in hand, and then he indeed comes.

He comes bowing and bending; he humbles himself greatly, makes supplication to the Lord, and prays to Him; and he was heard and had mercy upon him (2 Chronicles 30:10).

The thief on the cross initially mocked Jesus alongside his fellow criminal. However, he was one whom the Father had given to the Son, and therefore, "shall come" must intervene in his rebellious will.

As soon as he is addressed by that absolute promise, he quickly changes his attitude. He stops railing and begins to plead with the Son of God for mercy. "Lord," he says, "remember me when You come into Your kingdom" (Matthew 27:44; Luke 23:40-42).

Objection. You say they shall come, but what if they are blind and cannot see the way? Some are kept away from Christ, not only by their stubbornness but also by the blindness of their minds. If they are blind, how can they come?

Answer: The question is not whether they are blind, but whether they are within the reach and power of "shall come." If they are, then the Christ who said they shall come will provide them with sight, a guide, or both to bring them to Himself. "Must is for the king." If they shall come, they shall come. No obstacle will hinder them.

The darkness of the Thessalonians did not prevent them from being children of light. "I have come," said Christ, "that those who do not see may see." And if He says, "See, you blind who have eyes," who can stop it? (Ephesians 5:8; John 9:39; Isaiah 29:18; 43:8).

This promise, therefore, is a grand promise, containing within it all that is necessary for its complete fulfillment. They shall come. However, it is objected that they are blind. Yet, "shall come" remains unchanged and continues to declare, "They shall come to Me." Therefore, He says again, "I will bring the blind by a way they do not know; I will lead them in paths they have not known; I will make darkness light before them and crooked things straight. These things I will do for them, and I will not forsake them" (Isaiah 42:16).

Mark this: I will bring them, even if they are blind; I will lead them by a way they do not know; I will— I will; and therefore "they shall come to Me."

Objection. But what if they have sinned greatly and made themselves more abominable? What if they are the leading sinners in their county, town, or family?

Answer: What then? Shall that hinder the execution of "shall come"? It is not transgressions, nor sins, nor all their transgressions in all their sins that will prevent this promise from being fulfilled upon them, if they are given by the Father to Christ for salvation.

"In those days, and in that time," says the Lord, "the iniquity of Israel shall be sought for, and there shall be none; and the sins of Judah, and they shall not be found" (Jeremiah 50:20). This does not mean that they had no sins, for they were overflowing with transgressions (2 Chronicles 33:9; Ezekiel 16:48).

However, God would pardon, cover, hide, and remove them by virtue of His absolute promise, by which they are given to Christ for salvation. "And I will cleanse them from all their iniquity, by which they have sinned against Me; and I will pardon all their iniquities, by which they have transgressed against Me. And it shall be to Me a name of joy, a praise, and an honor before all the nations of the earth, which shall bear all the good that I do unto them; and they shall fear and tremble for all the goodness and for all the prosperity that I procure unto it" (Jeremiah 33:8-9).

Objection. But how can they come if they lack faith and repentance?

Answer: The one who says they shall come, will He not make it happen? If they shall come, they shall come. If faith and repentance are the means by which they come, as indeed they are, then faith and repentance shall be given to them! For "shall come" must be fulfilled in them.

Faith shall be given to them. "I will also leave in the midst of you an afflicted and poor people, and they shall trust in the name of the Lord." "There shall be a root of Jesse, and he who rises to reign over the Gentiles; in him shall the Gentiles trust" (Zephaniah 3:12; Romans 15:12).

They shall have repentance. He is exalted to give repentance. "They shall come weeping, and seeking the Lord their God." And again, "With weeping and supplication will I lead them" (Acts 5:31; Jeremiah 31:9).

I told you before that an absolute promise contains all conditional ones within it, along with the provision to meet all those qualifications that are proposed to Him who seeks their benefit. It must be so; for if "shall come" is an absolute promise, as it indeed is, then it must be fulfilled for everyone concerned.

I say it must be fulfilled if God can, by grace and His absolute will, accomplish it. Furthermore, since coming and believing are essentially the same, according to John 6:35, "He who comes to Me shall never hunger, and he who believes in Me shall never thirst," then when He says they shall come, it is as much as to say they shall believe, and consequently repent, to the saving of their souls.

Therefore, the current lack of faith and repentance cannot nullify this promise of God, because this promise includes the ability to provide what others call for and expect.

I will give them a heart, I will give them My Spirit, I will give them repentance, I will give them faith. Mark these words: "If anyone is in Christ, he is a new creation." But how did he become a "new creation," since none can create but God? Indeed, God makes them "new creations." "Behold," says He, "I make all things new."

Thus, it follows that even after stating they are "new creations," "all things are of God;" that is, all this new creation stands in the various operations and special workings of the Spirit of grace, who is God (2 Corinthians 5:17,18).

Objection. But how shall they escape all those dangerous and damnable opinions that, like rocks and quicksands, lie in the way they are going?

Answer: Indeed, this age is filled with errors, perhaps more than any other age in history. Yet, the gift of the Father, claimed by the Son in the text, must surely lead them to escape these errors and ultimately come to Him.

There are a number of "shall comes" in the Bible that secure them. They may be assaulted by these errors and even become entangled and detained by them from the Bishop of their souls, but these "shall comes" will break the chains and fetters that those given to Christ are caught in, and they shall come because He has said they shall come to Him.

Indeed, errors are like that woman described in Proverbs, who sits in her seat in the high places of the city, "to call passengers who go right on their ways" (Proverbs 9:13-16). However, the individuals that the Father has given to the Son for salvation will, at one time or another, be secured by the promise of "shall come to Me."

Therefore, it is said that God will guide them with His eye, with His counsels, by His Spirit, and in the way of peace; by the springs of water, and into all truth (Psalm 32:8; 73:24; John 16:13; Luke 1:79; Isaiah 49:10).

So, he who has such a guide, and all that the Father gives to Christ shall have it, will escape those dangers and will not err in the way. Yes, even if he is a fool, he will not err therein (Isaiah 35:8). For every such person it is said, "Your ears shall hear a word behind you, saying, This is the way, walk in it, when you turn to the right hand, and when you turn to the left" (Isaiah 30:21).

There were thieves and robbers before Christ's coming, as there are now; but, He said, "The sheep did not hear them." And why did they not hear them? Because they were under the power of "shall come," that absolute promise, which contained the grace to enable them to rightly distinguish voices. "My sheep hear My voice." But how did they come to hear it? To them it is given to know and to hear, and that distinctly (John 10:8,16; 5:25; Ephesians 5:14).

Furthermore, the very clear statement of the text provides against all these issues; for it says, "All that the Father gives Me shall come to Me;" that is, they shall not be stopped or be lured to settle anywhere short of Me, nor shall they turn aside to remain with anyone besides Me.

The significance of the words "Shall come TO ME" is profound. By these words, there is implied, though not explicitly stated, a dual reason for their coming to Him. First, there is in Christ a fullness of all-sufficiency, encompassing everything needed for our happiness. Second, those who truly come to Him do so in order to receive this fullness from His hand.

Firstly, regarding the first point, there is in Christ a fullness of all-sufficiency, which includes everything necessary to make us happy. As it is written, "For it pleased the Father that in Him all fullness should dwell" (Colossians 1:19). Furthermore, "Of His fullness we have all received, and grace for grace" (John 1:16). It is also stated that His riches are unsearchable: "the unsearchable riches of Christ" (Ephesians 3:8). Listen to what He says of Himself: "Riches and honor are with me; durable riches and righteousness. My fruit is better than gold, yes, than fine gold; and my revenue than choice silver. I lead in the way of righteousness, in the midst of the paths of judgment; that I may cause those who love me to inherit substance. And I will fill their treasures" (Proverbs 8:18-21).

This is a general overview. More specifically, there is a light in Christ that is sufficient to lead them out of, and away from, all the darkness in which others, except those who come to Him, stumble, fall, and perish. He declares, "I am the light of the world."

He states, "He who follows me shall not walk in darkness, but shall have the light of life" (John 8:12). By nature, man is in darkness, walking in darkness, and does not know where he is going, for darkness has blinded his eyes. Nothing but Jesus Christ can lead men out of this darkness. Natural conscience cannot do it; the Ten Commandments, although present in the heart of man, cannot do it. This privilege belongs solely to Jesus Christ.

There is also a life in Christ that cannot be found anywhere else (John 5:40). This life acts as a principle in the soul, enabling it to do what is pleasing to God through Him. He says, "He who believes in me, as the Scripture has said, out of his belly shall flow rivers of living water" (John 7:38). Without this life, a person is dead, whether they are considered good or bad in their own eyes or in the eyes of others. There is no true and eternal life except what is found in the ME that speaks in the text.

There is also life for those who come to Him, available through faith in

His flesh and blood. "He who eats me, even he shall live by me" (John 6:57). This life counters the death that comes from the guilt of sin and the curse of the law, under which all men are bound and must remain unless they partake of the ME that speaks in the text. "Whoever finds ME," He says, "finds life;" deliverance from everlasting death and destruction, which, without me, will consume him (Proverbs 8:35). Nothing is more desirable than life to one who bears the sentence of condemnation; and here alone is life to be found. This life, namely eternal life, is in His Son; that is, in Him who says in the text, "All that the Father has given me shall come to me" (1 John 5:10).

The person speaking in the text is the only one through whom poor sinners have access to and acceptance with the Father, due to the glory of His righteousness. In Him, they are presented as amiable and spotless in His sight; there is no other way to come to the Father except through Him. "I am the way," He says, "the truth, and the life; no one comes to the Father except through me" (John 14:6). All other paths to God are dead and damnable; the flaming cherubim stand guard with swords, turning every way to keep all others from His presence (Genesis 3:24). I assert that this applies to all except those who come through Him. "I am the door; by me," He says, "if anyone enters in, he shall be saved" (John 10:9).

The person speaking in the text is HE, and only HE, who can provide stable and everlasting peace. Therefore, He says, "My peace I give unto you." This peace is a peace with God, a peace of conscience, and one that lasts forever. My peace, which cannot be matched, is "not as the world gives;" for the world's peace is merely carnal and temporary, but mine is Divine and eternal. Hence, it is called the peace of God, which surpasses all understanding.

The person speaking in the text possesses enough of all things that are truly spiritually good to satisfy the desires of every longing soul. "Jesus stood and cried, saying, If anyone thirsts, let him come to me and drink." And to the thirsty, "I will give of the fountain of the water of life freely" (John 7:37; Revelation 21:6).

With the person speaking in the text is the power to perfect, defend, and deliver those who come to Him for safety. "All power," He says, "is given unto me in heaven and on earth" (Matthew 28:18).

Thus might I multiply instances of this nature in abundance.

But, second, those who truly come to Him do so in order to receive from His hand. They come for light, they come for life, they come for reconciliation with God. They also come for peace; they come so that their souls may be satisfied with spiritual good and that they may be protected by Him against all spiritual and eternal damnation. He alone is able to give them all this, filling their joy to the full, as they discover when they come to Him. This is evident from the plain declaration of those who have already come to Him: "Being justified by faith, we have peace with God through our Lord Jesus Christ, through whom also we have access by faith into this grace in which we stand, and rejoice in hope of the glory of God" (Romans 5:1-2).

It is also evident that while they keep their eyes upon Him, they never desire to exchange Him for another or to add anything else to themselves alongside Him to complete their spiritual joy. "God forbid," says Paul, "that I should glory, except in the cross of our Lord Jesus Christ." "Indeed, I count all things as loss for the excellence of the knowledge of Christ Jesus my Lord. For whom I have suffered the loss of all things, and count them as rubbish, that I may gain Christ and be found in Him, not having my own righteousness, which is from the law, but that which is through faith in Christ, the righteousness which is from God by faith" (Philippians 3:8-9).

It is also evident by their earnest desires that others might partake in their blessedness. "Brethren," said Paul, "my heart's desire and prayer to God for Israel is that they might be saved." This is the same way he expected to be saved himself. As he also says to the Galatians, "Brethren, I beseech you, be as I am; for I am as you are." That is, I am a sinner just like you. Now, I urge you to seek for life, as I am seeking it; for there is sufficiency in the Lord Jesus for both me and you.

It is also evident by the triumph that such individuals have over all their enemies, both bodily and spiritual: "Now thanks be to God," said Paul, "who always leads us in triumph in Christ." And, "Who shall separate us from the love of Christ our Lord?" Again, "O death, where is your sting? O grave, where is your victory? The sting of death is sin, and the strength of sin is the law; but thanks be to God, who gives us the victory through our Lord Jesus Christ" (2 Corinthians 2:14; Romans 8:35; 1 Corinthians 15:55-56).

It is also evident that they are made by the glory of what they have found in Him to endure whatever the devil and hell itself may devise to separate them from Him. Again, "Who shall separate us from the love of Christ? Shall tribulation, or distress, or persecution, or famine, or nakedness, or peril, or sword? As it is written, 'For Your sake we are killed all day long; we are accounted as sheep for the slaughter.' Nay, in all these things we are more than conquerors through Him who loved us. For I am persuaded that neither death, nor life, nor angels, nor principalities, nor powers, nor things present, nor things to come, nor height, nor depth, nor any other creature shall be able to separate us from the love of God which is in Christ Jesus our Lord" (Romans 8:35-39).

"Shall come TO ME." Oh, the heart-attracting glory that is in Jesus Christ when He is revealed, drawing those to Him who are given to Him by the Father. Therefore, those who came in the past expressed this as the reason for their coming to Him: "And we beheld His glory, the glory as of the only begotten of the Father" (John 1:14). The reason why others do not come but perish in their sins is due to a lack of sight of His glory: "If our gospel is hidden, it is hidden to those who are lost; in whom the god of this world has blinded the minds of those who do not believe, lest the light of the glorious gospel of Christ, who is the image of God, should shine on them" (2 Corinthians 4:3-4).

There is, therefore, heart-pulling glory in Jesus Christ, which, when revealed, draws the person to Him. Thus, when His glory is revealed, they must come; they shall come to Him. Therefore, as the true seekers come with weeping and repentance, being aware of their own vileness, it is also said that "the ransomed of the Lord shall return and come to Zion with songs and everlasting joy upon their heads; they shall obtain joy and gladness, and sorrow and sighing shall flee away." This is at the sight of the glory of that grace which now shows itself to them in the face of our Lord Jesus Christ, and in the hopes they now have of being with Him in the heavenly tabernacles. Therefore, it is said again, "With gladness and rejoicing shall they be brought; they shall enter into the King's palace" (Isaiah 35:10; 51:11; Psalm 45:15). There is, therefore, heart-attracting glory in the Lord Jesus Christ, which, when revealed, subjects the heart to the Word and compels us to come to Him.

It is said of Abraham that when he lived in Mesopotamia, "the God of glory appeared to him," saying, "Get out of your country." And what happened then? He left his home and friends, and nothing in the world could stop him.

"Now," as the Psalmist asks, "Who is this King of glory?" he answers, "The Lord, mighty in battle" (Psalm 24:8). And who is that, but the one who "spoiled principalities and powers" when He hung upon the tree, triumphing over them there? That is none other than Jesus Christ, the very person speaking in the text. Therefore, it is said of Abraham, "He saw His day. Yes," He said to the Jews, "your father Abraham rejoiced to see My day, and he saw it and was glad" (Colossians 2:15; James 2:23; John 8:56).

Indeed, the carnal man says, at least in his heart, "There is no form or comeliness in Christ; and when we see Him, there is no beauty that we should desire Him" (Isaiah 53:2); but he lies. He speaks this as one who has never seen Him. However, those who stand in His house and look upon Him through the glass of His Word, with the help of His Holy Spirit, will tell you otherwise. "But we all," they say, "with unveiled face, beholding as in a mirror the glory of the Lord, are transformed into the same image from glory to glory" (2 Corinthians 3:18). They see glory in His person, glory in His works, glory in the merit of His blood, and glory in the perfection of His righteousness; indeed, heart-affecting, heart-sweetening, and heart-changing glory!

Indeed, His glory is veiled and cannot be seen except as revealed by the Father (Matthew 11:27). It is concealed by flesh, by the lowliness of His earthly lineage, and by the ignominy and shame that accompanied Him in the flesh. However, those who can, in God's light, see beyond these things will behold glory in Him—such glory that will draw and captivate their hearts to Him.

Moses was the adopted son of Pharaoh's daughter, and for all I know, he might have become king in the end if he had conformed to the current vanities present at court. However, he could not, and he would not do it.

Why? What was the matter? The reason is that he saw more in the worst of Christ (bear with the expression) than he saw in the best of all the treasures of the land of Egypt. He "refused to be called the son of Pharaoh's daughter, choosing rather to suffer affliction with the people of God than to enjoy the pleasures of sin for a season. He esteemed the reproach of Christ greater riches than the treasures in Egypt, for he had respect unto the recompense of the reward. He forsook Egypt, not fearing the wrath of the king."

But what emboldened him to do this? The answer is that "he endured," for he had a vision of the person speaking in the text. "He endured, as seeing Him who is invisible."

But I ask, would a sight of Jesus have so taken Moses' heart away from a crown and a kingdom if he had not, by that sight, seen more in Him than was to be seen in those worldly treasures? (Hebrews 11:24-26).

Therefore, when He says, "shall come to Me," He means that they shall have a revelation of the glory of the grace that is in Him. The beauty and glory of that grace are of such virtue that they compel and draw the hearts of those who are given to Him with a blessed force.

Moses, whom we spoke of earlier, was not a child when he was captivated by the beautiful glory of his Lord. He was forty years old, and thus, being a man of wisdom and opportunity, he was able to make the best judgment of the things and their goodness that lay before him in the land of Egypt. Yet, he was the one who set a low esteem upon the glory of Egypt, counting it not worth pursuing when he had a vision of the Lord Jesus Christ. This wicked world thinks that the idea of heaven and happiness in the afterlife may suffice to capture the hearts of those who either lack the world's good things to delight in or are foolish and do not know how to enjoy them. But let them know that we have had men of all ranks and qualities who have been captivated by the glory of our Lord Jesus and have left everything to follow Him. As Abel, Seth, Enoch, Noah, Abraham, Isaac, Jacob, Moses, Samuel, David, Solomon; and who else, that had either wisdom or grace to savor heavenly things? Indeed, no one can resist Him or hold out against Him to whom He reveals the glory of His grace.

8. Christ's Promise to All Who Come to Him

"And him that comes to me I will in no wise cast out."

With these words, our Lord Jesus expresses even more fully the great goodness of His nature toward the coming sinner. Previously, He said, "They shall come"; here He declares that He will receive them with heart and affection. However, let me address the seeming conditionality of this promise. "And him that comes to Me I will in no wise cast out." Some may say that Christ's acceptance of us depends on our coming, thus making our salvation conditional. If we come, we shall be received; if not, we shall not be, as the words imply. The promise of acceptance is only to him that comes. "And him that comes." I respond that the coming mentioned here, as a condition for being received to life, is something promised and concluded to be accomplished in us by the preceding promise. In the latter words, coming to Christ is implicitly required of us; and in the earlier words, that grace which enables us to come is positively promised to us. "All that the Father gives Me shall come to Me; and him that comes to Me I will in no wise cast out." We come to Christ because it is said, "We shall come"; because it is given to us to come. Thus, the condition expressed by Christ in these latter words is absolutely promised in the preceding words. Indeed, the coming intended here is nothing but the effect of "shall come to Me. They shall come, and I will not cast them out."

"And Him That Comes."

He does not say, "and him that is come," but "him that comes." To elaborate on these words, I will first address them in general, and then more particularly.

[First] In general. These words suggest four things:

1. That Jesus Christ builds upon the fact that since the Father gave His people to Him, they shall be enabled to come to Him. "And him that

comes." As if to say, "I know that since they are given to Me, they shall be enabled to come to Me." He does not say, "if they come," or "I suppose they will come," but "and him that comes." Therefore, He shows us that He prepares Himself to receive those whom the Father gave Him to save. He is ready to embrace them, expecting that the Father will bring them into His bosom.

Christ also implies through these words that He knows very well who are given to Him—not by their coming to Him, but by their being given to Him. "All that the Father gives Me shall come to Me; and him that comes," etc. This individual is known to Him as one of those whom the Father has given Him; therefore, He receives him because the Father has given him to Him (John 10). "I know My sheep," He says. Not only those who already know Him but also those who are still ignorant of Him. "Other sheep I have," He said, "which are not of this fold" (John 10:16); not of the Jewish church, but those who lie in their sins, even the rude and barbarous Gentiles. Therefore, when Paul was afraid to stay at Corinth, fearing some mischief might befall him there, the Lord Jesus said to him, "Be not afraid, but speak, and hold not your peace—for I have much people in this city" (Acts 18:9-10). The people the Lord speaks of were not yet considered His due to a previous work of conversion, but by virtue of the gift of the Father; for He had given them to Him. Thus, Paul was to remain there to speak the word of the Lord to them, so that through his speaking, the Holy Spirit might effectively work in their souls, causing them to come to Him, who was also ready, with heart and soul, to receive them.

Christ, by these words, also suggests that no one comes to Him except those who are given to Him by the Father. The "Him" in this context refers to the "all" that was mentioned earlier by Christ. "All that the Father gives Me shall come to Me; and the one who comes to Me I will by no means cast out." This is further implied by the apostle when he says, "He gave some to be apostles, some prophets, some evangelists, and some pastors and teachers, for the equipping of the saints, for the work of the ministry, for the edifying of the body of Christ; till we all come to the unity of the faith and of the knowledge of the Son of God, to a perfect man, to the measure of the stature of the fullness of Christ" (Ephesians 4:11-13).

Mark, as in the text, speaks of all. "Until we all come." We all! All who? Certainly, "All that the Father gives to Christ." This is further implied because he calls this "all" the body of Christ, the measure of the stature of the fullness of Christ. By this, he refers to the universal number given, namely, the true elect church, which is said to be His body and fullness (Ephesians 1:22-23).

Christ Jesus, by these words, further suggests that He is well pleased with this gift from the Father. "All that the Father gives Me shall come to Me; and the one who comes to Me I will by no means cast out." I will heartily, willingly, and with great contentment of mind, receive him.

They also show us that Christ's love in receiving is as vast as His Father's love in giving, and no larger. Hence, He thanks the Father for His gift and also for hiding Him and His things from the rest of the wicked (Matthew 11:25; Luke 10:21). But, secondly, and more specifically, "And HIM that comes."

The significance of the word "HIM" is that Christ looks back to the gift of the Father, not only in the entirety of the gift but to each individual "him" within that whole. As if to say, I do not only accept the gift of my Father in general, but I have a special regard for each one in particular; and I will secure not only some or the majority, but every single one, every individual. Not a hoof shall be lost or left behind. Indeed, in this, He consents to His Father's will, which is that of all that He has given Him, He should lose nothing (John 6:39).

"And him." Christ Jesus, by thus dividing the gift of His Father into individual "hims," and by referring to them in the singular, shows what a specific work shall be accomplished in each one at the time appointed by the Father. "And it shall come to pass in that day," says the prophet, "that the Lord shall beat off from the channel of the river to the stream of Egypt, and you shall be gathered one by one, O children of Israel."

Here are the "hims," one by one, to be gathered to Him by the Father (Isaiah 27:12).

He also shows that no lineage, kinship, or relation can benefit from any outward or carnal union with the person that the Father has given to Christ. It is only the given "HIM," the coming "HIM," that He intends absolutely to secure. People often make a great fuss about the children of believers; but if the child of a believer is not the "HIM" concerned in this absolute promise, then neither the cries of these people nor what the parent or child can do will interest him in this promise of the Lord Christ.

"And Him"

There are various types of individuals that the Father has given to Jesus Christ; they are not all of the same rank or quality. Some are high, some are low; some are wise, some are foolish; some are more civil and compliant with the law, while others are more profane and averse to Him and His gospel. Now, since those given to Him are, in some sense, so diverse, and since He still says, "And him that comes," He indicates that He is not like men, who pick and choose, taking the best and leaving the worst. Rather, He is for the one that the Father has given Him and that comes to Him. "He shall not alter it, nor change it, a good for a bad, or a bad for a good" (Leviticus 27:10); but will take him as he is and will save his soul.

There are many sad wretches given by the Father to Jesus Christ; yet not one of them is despised or slighted by Him. It is said of those that the Father has given to Christ that they have done worse than the heathen; that they were murderers, thieves, drunkards, unclean persons, and more. Yet He has received them, washed them, and saved them. A fitting emblem of this is the wretched instance mentioned in the sixteenth chapter of Ezekiel, where a child was cast out in a loathsome condition at birth; a creature in such a wretched state that no eye pitied it or showed compassion, except for His who speaks in the text.

"And Him"

Let him be as red as blood, let him be as red as crimson. Some people are blood-red sinners, crimson sinners, sinners of a double dye; dipped and dipped again before they come to Jesus Christ. Are you, dear reader, such a person? Speak up! Are you one of them? And are you now coming to Jesus Christ for the mercy of justification, so that you might be made white in His blood and covered with His righteousness? Fear not; for your coming indicates that you are among those whom the Father has given to Christ; He will in no wise cast you out. "Come now," says Christ, "and let us reason together; though your sins be as scarlet, they shall be as white as snow; though they be red like crimson, they shall be as wool" (Isaiah 1:18).

Many strange individuals came to Jesus Christ during his time on earth, and he received them all without turning anyone away.

He spoke to them about the kingdom of God and healed those who needed healing (Luke 9:11; 4:40). These words, "AND HIM," are indeed remarkable. Not one person who comes to Jesus Christ, drawn by the Father's gift, should be rejected or overlooked. Instead, they are welcomed to partake in his saving grace.

In Luke, it is said that the people "wondered at the gracious words which proceeded out of his mouth" (4:22). These words are like drops of honey; as it is written, "Pleasant words are like a honeycomb, sweet to the soul and health to the bones" (Proverbs 16:24). These are truly gracious words, as full as a faithful and merciful High Priest could express.

Luther said, "When Christ speaks, he has a mouth as wide as heaven and earth." This means he speaks fully to encourage every sinful person coming to Jesus Christ. To confirm this, listen to his own words: "Heaven and earth will pass away, but my words will by no means pass away" (Isaiah 51:6; Matthew 24:35).

This is further confirmed by the testimonies of the four evangelists, who faithfully reported his loving reception of all kinds of sinners, whether they were tax collectors, prostitutes, thieves, possessed by demons, or otherwise troubled (Luke 19:1-10; Matthew 21:31; Luke 15; 23:43; Mark 16:9; 5:1-9).

This shows us:

1. The greatness of Christ's merits.

2. The willingness of his heart to grant life to great sinners who come to him.

This illustrates the greatness of Christ's merits. We should not assume that his words are greater than his worthiness. He is powerful enough to fulfill his promises. He can do exceedingly abundantly more than we ask or think, even beyond what we can imagine (Ephesians 3:20). Therefore, since he welcomes any person who comes to him, we can conclude that he is able to save to the uttermost any sinner who approaches him.

Do you think the Lord Jesus did not consider his words before he spoke? He speaks in righteousness, and through his words, we can understand how mighty he is to save (Isaiah 63:1). He speaks in righteousness and faithfulness when he began to build this blessed gospel. He first sat down and counted the cost, knowing he was able to complete it!

What about you, Lord? Any person who comes to you? This is a Christ worth seeking; this is a Christ worth coming to!

This should teach us to carefully consider the true power of every word of God. We should evaluate Christ's ability to save not by our sins or our limited understanding of his grace, but by his word, which is the true measure of grace. If we do not judge in this way, we will dishonor his grace, miss the benefits of his word, and unnecessarily frighten ourselves with discouragements when coming to Jesus Christ.

To any person who comes, there is enough in this word of Christ to nourish hope for salvation. As you approach, coming sinner, consider whether Christ can save you based on the true meaning of his words. Reflect on the efficacy of his blood, the perfection of his righteousness, and the power of his intercession, as expressed in his word. "And him," he says, "who comes to me I will by no means cast out." "By no means," that is, for no sin. Therefore, judge by his word how capable he is to save you. It is said of God's promises to the children of Israel, "There failed not a single good thing which the Lord had spoken to the house of Israel; all came to pass" (Joshua 21:45). Again, "Not one thing has failed of all the good things which the Lord your God spoke concerning you; all have come to pass, and not one thing has failed" (Joshua 23:14).

Coming sinner, whatever promise you find in the word of Christ, hold onto it as tightly as you can, as long as you do not distort it. His blood and merits will fulfill all that the word states or any true conclusion drawn from it. You may boldly rely on it. In the text, he says, "And him that comes," without any indication of rejecting anyone, no matter how great their sins, if they are a coming sinner.

Take it as a given that you, whoever you are, if you are coming, are included in these words. It will not harm Christ at all if, like Benhadad's servants who served Ahab, you take him at his word. "Now," the text says, "the man diligently observed whether anything would come from him," meaning any word of grace, "and he hastily caught it."

It happened that Ahab had called Benhadad his brother. The man replied, "Your brother Benhadad!" (1 Kings 20:33), catching him at his word. Sinner, coming sinner, serve Jesus Christ in this way, and he will appreciate it. When he referred to the Canaanite woman as a dog, she caught him at his words and said, "Truth, Lord; yet the dogs eat of the crumbs which fall from their master's table." She caught him in his words, and he responded kindly, saying, "O woman, great is your faith; be it unto you even as you will" (Matthew 15:28).

Catch him, coming sinner; catch him in his words. Surely he will take it kindly and will not be offended by you.

The other point I mentioned is this: The willingness of Christ's heart to grant his merits for life to great sinners who come to him. "And him that comes to me I will in no wise cast out."

The awakened coming sinner does not easily question Christ's power, but rather his willingness to save him. "Lord, if you are willing, you can," said one (Mark 1:40). He did not doubt Christ's power but questioned his willingness. He believed that Christ could save him but was not fully convinced that he would.

However, we have the same basis to believe that he will as we do to believe that he can. Indeed, we have grounds for both in the Word of God. If he were not willing, why did he make a promise? Why did he say he would receive the coming sinner?

Coming sinner, take note of this: we often plead our cases with men, so why not with God as well? We have no more basis for one than the other, as we must plead the promise of a faithful God. Jacob did this: "You said," he reminded God, "I will surely do you good" (Genesis 32:12). From this promise, he concluded that it followed logically that "He must be willing."

The text also provides grounds for us to draw the same conclusion: "And him that comes to me I will by no means cast out." Here, his willingness is asserted, as well as his power suggested.

It is worth noting that Abraham's faith considered God's power more than his willingness. He concluded, "I shall have a child," based on God's ability to fulfill the promise made to him. He believed that God was willing to give him a child; otherwise, God would not have promised one. "He did not waver at the promise of God through unbelief, but was strengthened in faith, giving glory to God, and being fully convinced that what He had promised, He was also able to perform" (Romans 4:20-21).

But was not his faith also tested regarding God's willingness? No, there was no reason to doubt that, because God had promised it. Indeed, had He not promised it, Abraham might have had a valid reason to doubt; but since He had made a promise, there was no ground for doubt left, as God's willingness to give a son was demonstrated in His promise.

These words, therefore, provide sufficient encouragement for any coming sinner that Christ is willing and able to receive him. Since He has the power to do what He wills, there is no reason left for the coming sinner to doubt. Instead, they should come with full hope of acceptance and grace.

"And him that comes." He does not say, "and him that has come," but "and him that comes" — that is, him whose heart begins to move toward me, who is leaving all for my sake; him who is looking out, who is on his journey to me. We must, therefore, distinguish between coming and having come to Jesus Christ. He who has come to Him has attained more of what he felt he needed than he who is still coming.

A man who has come to Christ has advantages over one who is still coming, and these can be outlined in seven ways.

He who has come to Christ is nearer to Him than he who is still coming. The one who is still coming is, in some sense, at a distance from Him, as it is said of the prodigal son, "And while he was still a great way off" (Luke 15:20).

Now, he who is nearer to Christ has the best view of Him and is able to make the best judgment of His wonderful grace and beauty. As God says, "Let them come near, then let them speak" (Isaiah 41:1). The Apostle John also states, "And we have seen and testify that the Father has sent the Son to be the Savior of the world" (1 John 4:14).

He who has not yet come, though he is coming, is not in a position to judge the worth and glory of Christ's grace as one who has already come to Him and has seen and experienced it. Therefore, sinner, hold your judgment until you are nearer.

He who has come to Christ has the advantage of being relieved of his burden. The one who is still coming has not yet been relieved of his burden (Matthew 11:28).

He who has come has cast his burden upon the Lord. By faith, he has seen himself released from it; but the one who is still coming feels the weight of it on his shoulders. "Come to Me, all you who labor and are heavy laden," implies that their burden, even while they are coming, is still upon them, and will remain until they truly come to Him.

He who has come to Christ has the advantage of having tasted the sweet and soul-refreshing water of life, while the one who is still coming has not. "If anyone thirsts, let him come to Me and drink" (John 7:37).

Note that he must come to Him before he drinks. As the prophet says, "Ho! Everyone who thirsts, come to the waters." He does not drink as he comes, but when he has come to the waters (Isaiah 55:1).

He who has come to Christ is not as terrified by the noise and the cries of the avenger of blood that pursue the one who is still coming. When the slayer was fleeing to the city of refuge, he faced the fear of the avenger of blood at his heels; but once he arrived in the city, that fear ceased.

In the same way, the one who is still coming to Jesus Christ hears many dreadful sounds in his ears—sounds of death and damnation—which the one who has come is currently free from. Therefore, He says, "Come, and I will give you rest." And again, "We who have believed enter that rest" (Hebrews 4).

Thus, he who has come to Christ is not as subject to the dejections and discouragements caused by the assaults of the evil one, as is the one who is still coming to Jesus Christ, even though he faces temptations too. "And while he was still coming, the devil threw him down and tormented him" (Luke 9:42).

For he who has come, despite Satan still roaring against him, possesses those experimental comforts and refreshments in his treasury to draw upon during times of temptation and conflict, which the one who is still coming does not have.

He who has come to Christ has the advantage of wearing the wedding garment, while the one who is still coming does not. The prodigal son, when he was coming home to his father, wore nothing but rags and was tormented by hunger. But when he arrived, the best robe was brought out, along with a gold ring and shoes, to his great joy. The fatted calf was killed for him, and music was played to celebrate his return. Thus, the Father Himself rejoiced, saying, "This my son was dead and is alive again; he was lost and is found" (Luke 15:18-19).

In summary, he who has come to Christ finds that his groans and tears, his doubts and fears, have been turned into songs and praises. He has now received the atonement and the earnest of his inheritance. In contrast, the one who is still coming does not yet have those praises or songs of deliverance, nor has he received the atonement and earnest of his inheritance, which includes the sealing testimony of the Holy Spirit through the sprinkling of the blood of Christ upon his conscience, for he has not yet come (Romans 5:11; Ephesians 1:13; Hebrews 12:22-24).

The significance of the word "COMETH" is profound. From this word, we can gather several important points:

Jesus Christ observes and takes note of the first stirrings of a sinner's heart as they seek Him. Coming sinner, you cannot desire Christ without Him noticing the movements of those desires within you. As David said, "All my desire is before You, and my groaning is not hidden from You" (Psalm 38:9). He spoke these words while he was coming back to the Lord after having backslidden.

It is noted that while the prodigal son was still a great distance away, his father saw him and recognized the longing in his heart (Luke 15:20).

When Nathanael approached Jesus Christ, the Lord said to those around Him, "Behold, an Israelite indeed, in whom is no guile." Nathanael responded, "How do You know me?" Jesus replied, "Before Philip called you, when you were under the fig tree, I saw you." I believe that at that moment, Nathanael was pouring out his soul to God, seeking mercy and understanding regarding the Messiah to come. Jesus saw all the workings of his sincere heart at that time (John 1:47-48).

Zacchaeus also experienced secret stirrings in his heart towards Jesus Christ when he ran ahead and climbed a tree to see Him. The Lord Jesus had His eye on him, and when He reached the spot, He looked up and said, "Zacchaeus, make haste and come down, for today I must stay at your house." This was to further complete the work of grace in Zacchaeus's soul (Luke 19:1-9). Remember this, coming sinner.

Just as Jesus Christ has His eye on the coming sinner, He also has His heart open to receive them. This is confirmed by the text: "And him who comes to Me I will in no wise cast out." His willingness to receive is further demonstrated by the way He prepares the path for the coming sinner, making it as easy as possible. This is evident in the blessed words, "I will in no wise cast out."

While the prodigal son was still a long way off, his father saw him, had compassion, ran to him, embraced him, and kissed him (Luke 15:20). All these expressions strongly affirm that Christ's heart is open to receive the coming sinner.

Jesus Christ has resolved that nothing will prevent Him from receiving the coming sinner. No sin of the sinner, nor the length of time spent in sin, will cause Jesus Christ to reject them.

Coming sinner, you are approaching a loving Lord Jesus!

These words were spoken from His blessed mouth to encourage the coming sinner to continue on their journey until they truly come to Jesus Christ. It was undoubtedly a great encouragement for blind Bartimaeus when Jesus stood still and called him while he was crying, "Jesus, Son of David, have mercy on me." Therefore, it is said that he cast away his garment, "rose, and came to Jesus" (Mark 10:46).

Now, if a call to come provides such encouragement, how much more encouraging is a promise of reception? Notice that although Bartimaeus had a call to come, without a promise, his faith had to rely on mere consequences, thinking, "He calls me; surely since He calls me, He will grant my desire."

Ah! But coming sinner, you do not need to go so far as to draw conclusions in this matter, for you have clear promises: "And him who comes to Me I will in no wise cast out." Here is full, plain, and abundant encouragement.

Suppose you were allowed to make a promise yourself, and Christ attested that He would fulfill it for the sinner who comes to Him. Could you create a better promise? Could you invent a more complete, free, or expansive promise? A promise that considers the first stirrings of the heart towards Jesus Christ? A promise that declares, and even engages, Christ Jesus to open His heart to receive the coming sinner?

Furthermore, a promise that demonstrates that the Lord Jesus is resolutely willing to receive and will in no wise cast out, nor intend to reject, the soul of the coming sinner! All of this is contained fully in this promise and flows naturally from it. You need not rely on far-fetched conclusions or strain your mind to extract encouraging arguments from the text. Coming sinner, the words are clear: "And him who comes to Me I will in no wise cast out."

9. Two Kinds of Sinners Who Come to Christ

There are two types of sinners who are coming to Jesus Christ.

1. The first is the one who has never, until recently, begun to come.

2. The second is the one who came in the past but then turned away, yet has since reconsidered and is now coming back.

Both types of sinners are included in the "him" of the text, as it is evident that both are now coming sinners. "And him who comes."

First. The newly-awakened comer.

Regarding the first type: the sinner who has recently begun to come, their path is easier. I do not mean to say it is more straightforward than the other; they do not bear the burden of a guilty conscience from backsliding.

However, all the encouragement of the gospel, along with the invitations it contains for coming sinners, is as free and open to one as it is to the other. Therefore, both can claim interest in the promise with the same freedom and liberty.

"All things are ready;" all things are prepared for the returning backsliders, just as they are for others: "Come to the wedding." "And let him who is thirsty come" (Matthew 22:1-4; Revelation 22:17).

Second. The returning backslider.

Having addressed the first type, I will now speak briefly to the one who is coming back to Jesus Christ for life after having backslidden.

Your way, O sinner of double guilt, is open to come to Jesus Christ. I refer to you, whose heart, after a long period of backsliding, is now considering returning to Him. Your way is as open as that of the other types of comers, as evidenced by what follows:

The text does not make any exceptions against you. It does not say, "And any him but a backslider." Rather, it opens its golden arms wide to every coming soul without exception. Therefore, you may come.

Be cautious not to close that door against your soul through unbelief, which God has opened by His grace.

The text is so far from excluding your coming that it strongly suggests you are one of the souls intended, O coming backslider. Why else would that clause, "I will in no wise cast out," have been included? It implies that even those who come now, having formerly backslidden, will not be cast away — neither the fornicator, the covetous, the railer, the drunkard, nor any other common sinner, nor the backslider themselves.

That the backslider is included is evident, for he is specifically mentioned by name: "Go, tell His disciples and Peter" (Mark 16:7). Peter was a godly man, true, but he was also a backslider — a desperate backslider. He had denied his Master once, twice, and even thrice, cursing and swearing that he did not know Him. If this is not backsliding, if this is not a significant and serious backsliding, then I have misjudged the matter.

Furthermore, when David had backslidden and committed adultery and murder during his backsliding, he was also sent to by name. The text states, "And the Lord sent Nathan to David." Nathan was sent to tell him, after David had sincerely acknowledged his sin, "The Lord has also put away, or forgiven your sin" (2 Samuel 12:1, 13).

This man was indeed far gone; he took another man's wife, killed her husband, and attempted to cover it all with wicked deceit. He did this after God had exalted him and shown him great favor. Therefore, his transgression was made even more grievous by the prophet, who highlighted its serious nature. Yet, he was accepted with joy at the very first step he took in returning to Christ. The first step of the backslider's return is to say, sincerely and unfeignedly, "I have sinned." No sooner had he said this than a pardon was offered to him, thrust into his bosom: "And Nathan said to David, The Lord has also put away your sin."

As the person of the backslider is mentioned by name, so too is his sin. This is done so that, if possible, your objections against returning to Christ may be removed. Your sin is mentioned by name and is intertwined with words of grace and favor: "I will heal their backsliding; I will love them freely" (Hosea 14:4). What do you say now, backslider?

Moreover, you are not only mentioned by name, and your sin by its nature, but you, as a returning backslider, are included: (a) Among God's Israel, "Return, O backsliding Israel, says the Lord; and I will not cause My anger to fall upon you; for I am merciful, says the Lord, and I will not keep anger forever" (Jeremiah 3:12). (b) You are included among His children, to whom He is married: "Turn, O backsliding children, for I am married to you" (verse 14). (c) After all this, as if His heart was so full of grace for them that He was compelled to express it, He adds, "Return, you backsliding children, and I will heal your backslidings" (verse 22).

Furthermore, the Lord understands that the shame of your sin has silenced you and made you almost prayerless. Therefore, He says to you, "Take with you words, and turn to the Lord: say to Him, 'Take away all iniquity, and receive us graciously.'" Consider His grace that He Himself would put words of encouragement into the heart of a backslider. As He states in another place, "I taught Ephraim to go, taking him by the arms." This is indeed teaching him to walk, to hold him up by the arms, as we say (Hosea 14:2; 11:3).

From what has been said, I conclude, as I stated before, that the "him" in the text, and "him that comes," includes both types of sinners.

Therefore, both should come freely.

Question: But where does Jesus Christ, in all the words of the New Testament, expressly speak to a returning backslider with words of grace and peace? What you have presented so far from the New Testament consists only of inferences drawn from this text. Indeed, it is a full text for carnal ignorant sinners who come, but to me, as a backslider, it offers little relief.

Answer: How can you say it offers little encouragement from the text when it states, "I will in no wise cast out"? What more could have been said? What is omitted here that might have been added to make the promise more complete and free? In fact, take all the promises in the Bible, all the freest promises, with all the variety of expressions of whatever nature or extent, and they can only amount to the essence of this very promise: "I will in no wise cast out." I will not, for any reason, by no means, upon no account, however they have sinned, however they have backslidden, however they have provoked, cast out the coming sinner.

Question: You ask, where does Jesus Christ, in all the words of the New Testament, speak to a returning backslider with words of grace and peace, specifically under the name of a backslider?

Answer: Where there are so many examples of receiving backsliders, there is less need for explicit words to that effect. One promise, like the text, along with the examples that accompany it, serves as a substitute for many promises. Moreover, I believe that the act of receiving is as much, if not more, encouraging than a mere promise to receive. Receiving is both the promise and its fulfillment; thus, in the Old Testament, you have the promise, and in the New Testament, you have its fulfillment, demonstrated through various examples.

In Peter, he denied his Master three times, even swearing an oath to do so. Yet, Christ received him again without any hesitation. Indeed, Peter stumbled and fell again, engaging in outright hypocrisy, which led to the downfall of many others. However, none of this served as a barrier to his salvation. Christ welcomed him back upon his return, as if He were unaware of Peter's faults (Galatians 2).

All the disciples, without exception, backslid and abandoned the Lord Jesus during His greatest trials. "Then all the disciples forsook Him and fled" (Matthew 26:56). They returned, as He had foretold, each to his own, leaving Him alone. Yet, Christ overlooked this as a minor issue. This was not because it was insignificant in itself, but rather due to the abundance of grace within Him, which allowed Him to dismiss it lightly. After His resurrection, when He first appeared to them, He did not rebuke them for their betrayal. Instead, He greeted them with words of grace, saying, "All hail! Be not afraid, peace be to you; all power in heaven and earth is given unto me." True, He did rebuke them for their unbelief, for that is what keeps us from Christ and His benefits (John 16:52; Matthew 28:9-11; Luke 24:39; Mark 16:14).

There was a man who, after making a large profession of faith, committed a grave sin by sleeping with his father's wife. This was a serious transgression, one that was not even heard of among the Gentiles at that time. Thus, this was a desperate backsliding. Yet, upon his return, he was received and accepted back into mercy (1 Corinthians 5:1-2; 2 Corinthians 2:6-8).

The thief who stole was instructed to steal no more, with no doubt that Christ was ready to forgive him for this act of backsliding (Ephesians 4:28).

All these examples serve as particular instances of Christ's willingness to receive backsliders into mercy. It is important to note that examples and proofs of His actions are stronger encouragements to our unbelieving hearts than mere promises that He will do so.

Moreover, the Lord Jesus has provided further encouragement for returning backsliders to come to Him.

1. He calls them to come, promising to receive them (Revelation 2:1-5; 14-16; 20-22; 3:1-3; 15-22). Thus, New Testament backsliders have ample encouragement to return.

2. He declares His readiness to receive those who come, as stated in the text and many other passages. Therefore, "Set up waymarks, make high heaps" of the golden grace of the gospel, and "set your heart toward the highway, even the way which you went." When you backslid, "turn again, O virgin of Israel, turn again to these your cities" (Jeremiah 31:21).

"And him that comes." He does not say, "and him that talks," "that professes," or "that makes a show." Rather, it is "him that comes." Christ will determine who among the many who make noise is truly coming to Him. It is not merely the one who claims to come, nor the one others affirm is coming; it is the one whom Christ Himself acknowledges as coming that is relevant in this text.

When the woman with the issue of blood approached Him for healing, many others thronged around Him, touching Him. However, Christ distinguished this woman from all the rest. "And He looked round about" to see her who had done this (Mark 5:25-32). He was not concerned with the thronging or touching of the others, as their actions were merely superficial or lacked the sincerity that made her touch acceptable. Therefore, Christ is the judge of who is genuinely coming to Him.

Every person believes their ways are right in their own eyes, "but the Lord weighs the spirits" (Proverbs 16:2). It is essential for everyone to be certain of their coming to Jesus Christ. For as your coming is, so shall your salvation be. If you come sincerely, your salvation will be genuine; but if you come only in outward appearance, your salvation will reflect that. For further discussion on coming, see the previous and subsequent sections on use and application.

"And him that comes TO ME." These words should be carefully noted.

They assure those who come to Him, while also warning against those who fall short in their coming and turn aside to others. It is important to understand that not everyone who comes is coming to Jesus Christ. Some come to Moses and his law, seeking life there; with these, Christ is not concerned, and His promise does not apply. "Christ has become of no effect to you; whoever of you is justified by the law, you have fallen from grace" (Galatians 5:4).

Others may come only as far as gospel ordinances and stop there, not progressing to Christ Himself. With these, He is also unconcerned; their "Lord, Lord" will not avail them anything on the great and dreadful day. A person may come to, and leave, the place and ordinances of worship, yet not be remembered by Christ. "So I saw the wicked buried," said Solomon, "who had come and gone from the place of the holy, and they were forgotten in the city where they had done so; this is also vanity" (Ecclesiastes 8:10).

"To me." These words are carefully chosen by Jesus Christ, serving both as a caution and an encouragement. They caution us not to settle for anything less than Christ in our coming. They encourage those who, in their coming, persevere until they reach Jesus Christ. "And him that comes to me I will in no wise cast out."

Reader, if you love your soul, take this caution from Jesus Christ to heart. You see your sickness, your wound, and your need for salvation. Do not go to King Jareb, for he cannot heal you or cure your wound (Hosea 5:13). Heed this warning, lest Christ, instead of being a Savior to you, becomes a lion, a young lion, ready to tear you apart and leave (Hosea 5:14).

There is a coming, but not to the Most High; there is a coming, but not with the whole heart, rather it is feigned. Therefore, take this caution to heart (Jeremiah 3:10; Hosea 7:16).

"And him that comes to me;" Christ, as a Savior, stands alone because His own arm alone has brought salvation. He will not be joined with

Moses, nor will He allow John the Baptist to share in His glory. They must vanish, for Christ will stand alone (Luke 9:28-36). Indeed, God the Father desires it this way; therefore, they must be separated from Him, and a voice from heaven must command the disciples to listen only to the beloved Son.

Christ will not allow any law, ordinance, statute, or judgment to partner with Him in the salvation of sinners. He does not say, "and him that comes to my WORD;" but rather, "and him that comes to ME." The words of Christ, even His most blessed and free promises, such as this one in the text, are not the Savior of the world; that role belongs solely to Christ Himself. The promises, therefore, exist to encourage the coming sinner to approach Jesus Christ and not to rest in them, falling short of salvation through Him.

The man who comes rightly casts all things behind him and does not look to or expect anything from anyone but the Son of God alone. As David said, "My soul, wait only upon God; for my expectation is from Him. He only is my rock and my salvation; He is my defense; I shall not be moved" (Psalm 62:5-6). His focus is on Christ, his heart is directed to Christ, and his expectation rests solely on Him.

Therefore, the man who comes to Christ is one who has deeply considered his own sins, has low thoughts of his own righteousness, and has high thoughts of the blood and righteousness of Jesus Christ. He sees, as I have mentioned, more virtue in the blood of Christ to save him than there is in all his sins to condemn him. He sets Christ before his eyes, knowing that there is nothing in heaven or earth that can save his soul and protect him from the wrath of God, except for Christ—specifically, His personal righteousness and blood.

The significance of the words "IN NO WISE" is profound. "And him that comes to Me, I will in no wise cast out."

"IN NO WISE": by these words, there is [First,] something expressed; and [Second,] something implied.

First, what is expressed is Christ Jesus' unchangeable resolution to save the coming sinner. He declares, "I will in no wise reject him or deny him the benefit of My death and righteousness." This phrase is akin to what He says about the everlasting damnation of the sinner in hellfire: "He shall by no means depart thence;" that is, he will never come out again, not for all eternity (Matthew 5:26; 25:46). Just as the condemned in hell have no hope for deliverance, so too does the one who comes to Christ have no reason to fear being cast out.

"Thus says the Lord, If heaven above can be measured, and the foundations of the earth searched out beneath, I will also cast off all the seed of Israel for all that they have done," says the Lord (Jeremiah 31:37). "Thus says the Lord, If My covenant is not with day and night, and if I have not appointed the ordinances of heaven and earth, then I will cast away the seed of Jacob" (Jeremiah 33:25-26).

However, heaven cannot be measured, nor can the foundations of the earth be searched out beneath; His covenant is also with day and night, and He has appointed the ordinances of heaven. Therefore, He will not cast away the seed of Jacob, who are the coming ones, but will certainly save them from the dreadful wrath to come (Jeremiah 50:4-5).

Thus, it is clear that it is not the greatness of sin, nor the long duration in it, nor even backsliding or the pollution of one's nature that can hinder the salvation of the coming sinner. If this were the case, then the solemn and absolute determination of the Lord Jesus would fall to the ground and be rendered ineffective. But His "counsel shall stand, and He will do all His pleasure;" that is, His pleasure in this matter, for His promise regarding this irreversible conclusion arises from His will; He will uphold it and fulfill it because it is His pleasure (Isaiah 46:10-11).

Suppose one man has sins, or as many sins as a hundred, and another has a hundred times as many; yet, if they both come, this word, "I will in no wise cast out," secures them both equally.

Suppose a man desires to be saved and is genuinely coming to Jesus Christ; however, he has led many to damnation through his debauched life. The door of hope is open for him by these words just as it is for someone who has not committed even a fraction of his transgressions. "And him that comes to Me I will in no wise cast out."

Suppose a man is coming to Christ to be saved and brings nothing but sin and a wasted life with him. Let him come, and welcome to Jesus Christ, "And he will in no wise cast him out" (Luke 7:42). Is not this love that surpasses knowledge? Is not this love a wonder to the angels? And is not this love worthy of acceptance by all coming sinners?

Hindrances in coming to Christ: Second, what is implied in these words is that the coming souls have those who continually lie in wait to have Jesus cast them off. The coming souls are afraid that these will prevail with Christ to cast them off. For these words are spoken to reassure us and to bolster our spirits against these two dangers: "I will in no wise cast out."

Coming souls have those who continually lie in wait to have Jesus Christ cast them off. There are three things that oppose the coming sinner.

First, there is the devil, that accuser of the brethren, who accuses them before God day and night (Revelation 12:10). This prince of darkness is tireless in this work; he does it, as you see, day and night, without ceasing. He continually presents his accusations against you, hoping to prevail. How did he work against that good man Job, attempting to bring about his destruction in hellfire? He argued that Job served God for nothing, tempting God to stretch out His hand against him, claiming that if He did, Job would curse Him to His face. All of this, as God testifies, he did without cause (Job 1:9-11; 2:4-5).

How did he also work against Christ with Joshua the high priest? "And he showed me Joshua," said the prophet, "the high priest, standing before the angel of the Lord, and Satan standing at his right hand to resist him" (Zechariah 3:1).

Satan stood there to resist him; that is, to persuade the Lord Jesus Christ to resist him, objecting to the uncleanness and unlawful marriages of his sons with the Gentiles, for that was the crime that Satan laid against them (Ezra 10:18).

Indeed, for all I know, Joshua may have been guilty of that very fact; but even if not, he was certainly guilty of crimes no less serious. He was clothed in filthy garments as he stood before the angel. He had no words to defend himself against all that this wicked one had to say against him. Yet, despite this, he was acquitted; he had a good Lord Jesus who did not resist him. Instead, He took up his cause, pleaded against the devil, excused his infirmity, and clothed him in justifying robes before his adversary's eyes.

"And the Lord said to Satan, 'The Lord rebuke you, O Satan! The Lord who has chosen Jerusalem rebuke you! Is this not a brand plucked from the fire?' And He spoke to those who stood before him, saying, 'Take away the filthy garments from him.' And to him He said, 'See, I have removed your iniquity from you, and I will clothe you with rich robes'" (Zechariah 3:2-4).

Again, how did Satan work against Peter when he desired to have him, that he might sift him as wheat? That is, if possible, to sever all grace from his heart and leave him with nothing but flesh and filth, so that he might make the Lord Jesus loathe and abhor him. "Simon, Simon," said Christ, "Satan has desired to have you, that he may sift you as wheat." But did he prevail against him? No. "But I have prayed for you, that your faith should not fail." As if to say, "Simon, Satan has desired that I would give you up to him, and not only you, but all the rest of your brethren— for that is what the word 'you' implies— but I will not leave you in his hand. I have prayed for you; your faith shall not fail; I will secure you for the heavenly inheritance" (Luke 22:30-32).

Just as Satan does, every sin of the coming sinner also raises a voice against him, hoping to persuade Christ to cast off the soul. When Israel was coming out of Egypt to Canaan, how many times had their sins cast them out of the mercy of God, had not Moses, as a type of Christ, stood in the breach to turn away His wrath from them! (Psalm 106:23). Our iniquities testify against us and would certainly prevail against us, leading to our utter rejection and damnation, had we not an advocate with the Father, Jesus Christ the righteous (1 John 2:1-2).

The sins of the old world cried them down to hell; the sins of Sodom brought down fire from heaven that consumed them; the sins of the Egyptians condemned them to hell because they did not come to Jesus Christ for life. Coming sinner, your sins are no less than theirs; indeed, they may be as great as all theirs. Why then do you live when they are dead, and why do you have a promise of pardon when they did not? "Why? Because you are coming to Jesus Christ;" therefore, sin shall not be your ruin.

Just as with Satan and sin, the law of Moses, being a perfect holy law, also has a voice against you before the face of God. "There is one who accuses you, even Moses," his law (John 5:45). Yes, it accuses all men of transgression who have sinned against it; for as long as sin is sin, there will be a law to accuse for sin. But this accusation shall not prevail against the coming sinner because it is Christ who died and who ever lives to make intercession for those who "come to God through Him" (Romans 8; Hebrews 7:25).

These things, I say, do accuse us before Christ Jesus; indeed, they also accuse us to our own faces, hoping to prevail against us. But these words, "I will in no wise cast out," secure the coming sinner from them all.

The coming sinner is not saved because there is no one who comes against him; rather, it is because the Lord Jesus will not listen to their accusations and will not cast out the coming sinner.

When Shimei came down to meet King David and sought pardon for his rebellion, Abishai immediately intervened, saying, "Shall not Shimei die for this?" This reflects the situation of anyone who comes to Christ. They have their own Abishai, and that Abishai steps in against them, saying, "Shall not this rebel's sins condemn him to hell?"

But David responded, "What have I to do with you, you sons of Zeruiah, that you should be adversaries to me today? Should any man be put to death in Israel today? For do I not know that I am king over Israel?" (2 Samuel 19:16-22).

This is Christ's answer to all who accuse the coming sinners. He says, "What have I to do with you, who accuse the coming sinners before me? I regard you as adversaries, opposing my mercy towards them. Do I not know that I am exalted today as the King of righteousness and the King of peace? I will in no wise cast them out."

However, these words imply that the coming souls are afraid these accusers will prevail against them. This is evident because the text is spoken for their relief and support. This need not be the case if those who are coming were not subject to fear and despair on this account. Alas, there is guilt, and the curse weighs heavily on the conscience of the coming sinner!

Moreover, he is aware of what a villain and wretch he has been against God and Christ. He now knows, through painful experience, how he has been at the beck and call of Satan and every lust. He also has new thoughts about the holiness and justice of God. He feels that he cannot refrain from sinning against Him. The motions of sin, which are by the law, still work in his members, bringing forth fruit unto death (Romans 7:5).

But none of this should discourage him since we have such a good, tender-hearted, and faithful Jesus to whom we can come. He would rather overthrow heaven and earth than allow a single word of this text to fail. "And him that comes to me I will in no wise cast out."

Now, we must inquire into two things that are found in these words, which have not yet been addressed. First, what it means to cast out. Second, how it is evident that Christ has the power to save or to cast out.

10. What It Means to Be Rejected by Christ

Regarding what it means to cast out. I will address this in two parts: First, generally. Second, more specifically.

First, generally. To cast out means to slight, despise, and contemptuously reject. As it is said of Saul's shield, "it was vilely cast away" (2 Samuel 1:21), meaning it was slighted and despised. Thus it is with sinners who do not come to Jesus Christ. He disregards, despises, and rejects them; that is, He "casts them away."

Things that are cast away are regarded as unclean rags and as the dirt of the street (Isaiah 3:24; Psalm 18:42; Matthew 5:13; 15:17). In this way, those who do not come to Jesus Christ will be counted as unclean and as dirt in the streets.

To be cast out or off means to be abhorred, not to be pitied, but to be subjected to perpetual shame (Psalm 44:9; 89:38; Amos 1:11). More specifically, the casting out mentioned here is not limited to this or that evil; it must be understood as extending to the most extreme and utmost misery. In other words, he who comes to Christ shall lack nothing that could make him spiritually happy in this world or in the world to come. Nor shall he lack anything that does not come to him, which could make him spiritually and eternally miserable. Furthermore, as it is to be generally understood concerning the things that are now, it also pertains to things that shall be hereafter.

For the things that are now can be categorized as either:

1. More general;

2. More particular.

More generally, thus:

"To be cast out" means to be excluded from the presence and favor of God. Thus was Cain cast out: "You have driven me out this day; from Your face I shall be hidden," meaning from Your favor (Genesis 4:14; Jeremiah 23:39; 1 Chronicles 28:9).

This is a dreadful complaint, but it is the result of an even more dreadful judgment.

"To be cast out" is to be removed from God's sight. God will no longer look after them, care for them, or watch over them for good (2 Kings 17:20; Jeremiah 7:15). Those who find themselves in this state are left like blind men, wandering and falling into the pit of hell. This, therefore, is also a sad judgment!

However, here lies the mercy for those who come to Christ. They shall not be left to wander in uncertainty. The Lord Jesus Christ will keep them, just as a shepherd keeps his sheep (Psalm 23). "Him that comes to me I will in no wise cast out."

"To be cast out" means to be denied a place in God's house, left as fugitives and vagabonds, passing a little time in this miserable life, and then going down to the dead (Galatians 4:30; Genesis 4:13-14; 21:10).

Therefore, here is the benefit for those who come to Christ: they shall not be denied a place in God's house. They will not be left like vagabonds in the world. "Him that comes to me I will in no wise cast out." See Proverbs 14:26, Isaiah 56:3-5, Ephesians 1:19-22, 1 Corinthians 3:21-23.

In summary, "to be cast out" is to be rejected like the fallen angels. Their eternal damnation began when they were cast down from heaven to hell. Therefore, not being cast out means having a place, a home, and a dwelling there, along with a share in the privileges of elect angels.

These words, therefore, "I will not cast out," will prove to be significant words one day for those who come to Jesus Christ (2 Peter 2:4; John 20:31; Luke 20:35).

Second, and more specifically, Christ has everlasting life for those who come to Him, and they shall never perish; "For He will in no wise cast him out." But for the rest, they are rejected, "cast out," and must face damnation (John 10:27-28).

Christ has everlasting righteousness to clothe those who come to Him, and they shall be covered with it like a garment. In contrast, the rest will be found in the filthy rags of their own sinful pollution and will be wrapped up in them, bearing their shame before the Lord and also before the angels (Daniel 9:27; Isaiah 57:20; Revelation 3:4-18, 15, 16).

Christ has precious blood that, like an open fountain, stands free for those who come to Him for life; "And He will in no wise cast him out." However, those who do not come to Him are rejected from sharing in it and are left to face the wrath for their sins (Zechariah 13:1; 1 Peter 1:18-19; John 13:8; 3:16).

Christ has precious promises, and those who come to Him for life shall share in them; for "He will in no wise cast them out." But those who do not come cannot share in these promises, as they are true only in Him; for in Him, and only in Him, all the promises are "yes" and "amen." Therefore, those who do not come to Him are not benefited by them at all (Psalm 50:16; 2 Corinthians 1:20-21).

Christ has fullness of grace in Himself for those who come to Him for life: "And He will in no wise cast them out." However, those who do not come to Him remain in their graceless state. As Christ leaves them, death, hell, and judgment find them. "Whoso findeth Me," says Christ, "findeth life, and shall obtain favor from the Lord. But he who sins against Me wrongs his own soul: all those who hate Me love death" (Proverbs 8:35-36).

Christ is an Intercessor who lives forever to make intercession for those who come to God through Him. However, their sorrows will be multiplied who chase after other gods or indulge in their sins and lusts. "I will not offer their drink offerings, nor take their names upon my lips" (Psalm 16:4; Hebrews 7:25).

Christ has wonderful love, compassion, and mercy for those who come to Him, for "He will in no wise cast them out." However, those who do not come to Him will find Him to be a lion ready to pounce; He will one day tear them to pieces. "Now consider this," He says, "you who forget God, lest I tear you in pieces, and there be none to deliver" (Psalm 50:22).

Christ is the one through whom those who come to Him have their persons and actions accepted by the Father. "And He will in no wise cast them out." In contrast, those who do not come to Him will seek refuge in the rocks and mountains, but it will be in vain, as they try to hide from His face and wrath (Revelation 6:15-17).

Furthermore, the phrase "CAST OUT" specifically refers to what will occur in the future, particularly on the day of judgment. It is then, and only then, that the great condemnation and casting out will be made evident, manifesting in execution. Therefore, I will address this under two main points: First, the act of casting out itself. Second, the place into which they will be cast.

First, the act of casting out consists of two elements:

1. A preparatory work.

2. The manner of executing the act.

The preparatory work consists of three aspects.

It involves the separation of those who have not come to Him from those who have, on that day. In other words, on the day of the great casting out, those who have not come to Him now will be separated from those who have; for those who have come to Him, "He will not cast out." "When the Son of Man comes in His glory, and all the holy angels with Him, then He will sit on the throne of His glory; and before Him will be gathered all nations, and He will separate them one from another, as a shepherd divides his sheep from the goats" (Matthew 25:31-32). This dreadful separation will then occur between those who come to Christ now and those who do not. It is only reasonable; since they would not come to Him while they had the opportunity, why should they stand with us when judgment comes?

They shall be placed before Him according to their condition. Those who have come to Him will be in great dignity, even at His right hand, for "He will in no wise cast them out." However, the rest shall be set at His left hand, the place of disgrace and shame, because they did not come to Him for life.

They will also be distinguished by appropriate terms. Those who come to Him are called His sheep, while the others are foolish goats. "And He shall separate them one from another, as a shepherd divides his sheep from the goats." The sheep will be set on His right hand, next to the gate of heaven, for they came to Him. In contrast, the goats will be on His left, destined to go from Him into hell, because they are not of His sheep.

Then Christ will proceed to convict those who did not come to Him, saying, "I was a stranger, and you did not take Me in," or "you did not come to Me." Their excuses will be dismissed as worthless, and He will proceed to their final judgment.

When these wretched rejecters of Christ are set before Him in their sins and convicted, this constitutes the preparatory work that precedes the manner of executing the act that will follow.

In the presence of all the holy angels.

In the presence of all those who, during their lifetime, came to Him, He will say to them, "Depart from Me, you cursed, into everlasting fire, prepared for the devil and his angels," along with the reason for this judgment. For you were cruel to Me and to those who belong to Me, as evidenced by these words: "For I was hungry, and you gave Me no food; I was thirsty, and you gave Me no drink; I was a stranger, and you did not take Me in; naked, and you did not clothe Me; sick, and in prison, and you did not visit Me" (Matthew 25:41-43).

Second, we must now discuss the place into which these shall be cast, which you have already heard described in general as the place prepared for the devil and his angels. Specifically, it is described as follows: It is called Tophet: "For Tophet is ordained of old, yes, for the king," referring to Lucifer. "It is prepared; He has made it deep and large; the pile thereof is fire and much wood; the breath of the Lord, like a stream of brimstone, does kindle it" (Isaiah 30:32).

It is called hell. "It is better for you to enter into life maimed, rather than having two hands, to go to hell" (Mark 9:45).

It is called the winepress of the wrath of God. "And the angel thrust in his sickle into the earth, and gathered the vine of the earth," referring to those who did not come to Christ, "and cast it into the great winepress of the wrath of God" (Revelation 14:19).

It is called a lake of fire. "And anyone not found written in the Book of Life was cast into the lake of fire" (Revelation 20:15).

It is called a pit. "You have said in your heart, 'I will ascend into heaven, I will exalt my throne above the stars of God; I will sit also upon the mount of the congregation, on the farthest sides of the north.' Yet you shall be brought down to hell, to the sides of the pit" (Isaiah 14:13-15).

It is called a bottomless pit, from which smoke and locusts came, and into which the great dragon was cast. It is referred to as bottomless to illustrate the endlessness of the fall for those who do not come to Jesus Christ in the acceptable time (Revelation 9:1-2; 20:3).

It is called outer darkness. "Bind him hand and foot, and cast him into outer darkness," and "cast the unprofitable servant into outer darkness; there will be weeping and gnashing of teeth" (Matthew 22:13; 25:30).

It is called a furnace of fire. "As therefore the tares are gathered and burned in the fire, so it will be at the end of this age. The Son of Man will send forth His angels, and they will gather out of His kingdom all things that offend, and those who practice lawlessness, and will cast them into the furnace of fire: there will be wailing and gnashing of teeth." Again, "So it will be at the end of the age: the angels will come forth, separate the wicked from among the just, and cast them into the furnace of fire: there will be wailing and gnashing of teeth" (Matthew 13:40-51).

Lastly, it may not be inappropriate, in concluding this, to briefly show what the things that torment them in this state are compared to. Indeed, some of them have been mentioned already; for instance, they are compared to wood that burns.

To fire and brimstone. However, it is also compared to a worm—a gnawing worm, a never-dying gnawing worm. They are cast into hell, "where their worm dieth not" (Mark 9:44).

It is called unquenchable fire. "He will gather His wheat into the garner; but He will burn up the chaff with unquenchable fire" (Matthew 3:12; Luke 3:17).

It is called everlasting destruction. "The Lord Jesus shall be revealed from heaven with His mighty angels in flaming fire, taking vengeance on them that know not God, and that obey not the gospel of our Lord Jesus Christ; who shall be punished with everlasting destruction from the presence of the Lord, and from the glory of His power" (2 Thessalonians 1:7-9).

It is called wrath without mixture, given to them in the cup of His indignation. "If any man worship the beast and his image, and receive his mark in his forehead or in his hand, the same shall drink of the wine of the wrath of God, which is poured out without mixture into the cup of His indignation; and he shall be tormented with fire and brimstone in the presence of the holy angels, and in the presence of the Lamb" (Revelation 14:9-10).

It is called the second death. "And death and hell were cast into the lake of fire. This is the second death. Blessed and holy is he who has part in the first resurrection: on such the second death has no power" (Revelation 20:6,14).

It is called eternal damnation. "But he who blasphemes against the Holy Spirit never has forgiveness, but is in danger of eternal damnation." Oh! These three words! Everlasting punishment! Eternal damnation! And forever and ever! How will they gnaw and consume all hope of an end to the misery of the castaway sinners? "And the smoke of their torment ascends up forever and ever; and they have no rest day or night" (Revelation 14:11).

Their behavior in hell is described by four things, as I know of:

1. By calling for help and relief in vain;

2. By weeping;

3. By wailing;

4. By gnashing of teeth.

11. Christ's Power to Save or Reject

Now we come to the second thing that needs to be inquired into, namely, how it appears that Christ has the power to save or to cast out. By these words, "I will in no wise cast out," He declares that He has the power to do both. This inquiry allows us to explore the following:

1. How it appears that He has the power to save;

2. How it appears that He has the power to cast out.

First, the fact that He has the power to save is evident from what follows. To speak only of Him as He is the mediator, He was authorized to this blessed work by His Father before the world began. Hence, the apostle says, "He has chosen us in Him before the foundation of the world" (Ephesians 1:4). This includes all those things that will effectively produce our salvation. Read the same chapter along with 2 Timothy 1:9.

He was promised to our first parents that He would, in the fullness of time, bruise the serpent's head. As Paul explains, He would redeem those who were under the law. Since that time, He has been regarded as slain for our sins. By this means, all the fathers under the first testament were secured from the wrath to come. Hence, He is called "The Lamb slain from the foundation of the world" (Revelation 13:8; Genesis 3:15; Galatians 4:4-5).

Moses gave testimony of Him through the types and shadows, and the bloody sacrifices that he commanded from the mouth of God to be used for the support of His people's faith until the time of reformation, which was the time of this Jesus' death (Hebrews 9, 10).

At the time of His birth, it was testified of Him by the angel, "That He should save His people from their sins" (Matthew 1:21).

It is testified of Him in the days of His flesh that He had power on earth to forgive sins (Mark 2:5-12).

It is also testified of Him by the apostle Peter that "God has exalted Him to His own right hand, to be a Prince and a Savior, to give repentance to Israel and forgiveness of sins" (Acts 5:31).

In summary, this is testified of Him everywhere, both in the Old Testament and the New. It is only reasonable that He should be acknowledged and trusted as a Savior.

He came down from heaven to be a Savior (John 6:38-40).

He was anointed while on earth to be a Savior (Luke 3:22).

He performed the works of a Savior. For example, (a) He fulfilled the law and became the end of it for righteousness for those who believe in Him (Romans 10:3-4).

He laid down His life as a Savior; He gave His life as "a ransom for many" (Matthew 20:28; Mark 10:45; 1 Timothy 2:6).

He has abolished death, destroyed the devil, put away sin, obtained the keys of hell and death, ascended into heaven, and is accepted by God. He is seated at the right hand as a Savior because His sacrifice for sins pleased God (2 Timothy 1:10; Hebrews 2:14-15; 10:12-13; Ephesians 4:7-8; John 16:10-11; Acts 5:30-31).

God has sent out and proclaimed Him as a Savior, telling the world that we have redemption through His blood. He will justify us if we believe in His blood, and He can do this faithfully and justly.

Indeed, God beseeches us to be reconciled to Him through His Son, which could not be if He were not anointed for this very purpose. It also could not be if His works and undertakings were not accepted by Him as a Savior (Romans 3:24-25; 2 Corinthians 5:18-21).

God has already received millions of souls into His paradise because they have accepted Jesus as their Savior.

He is determined to cut off and cast out of His presence those who will not accept Him as their Savior (Hebrews 12:22-26).

I intend to be brief here; therefore, I will say a word about the second point and conclude.

Second, it is evident that He has the power to cast out. This is shown by what follows:

The Father, for the service that He has done as Savior, has made Him Lord of all, even Lord of the living and the dead. "For to this end Christ both died, and rose, and revived, that He might be Lord both of the dead and living" (Romans 14:9).

The Father has entrusted Him with the authority to give life to whom He wills, specifically with saving grace, and to cast out whom He wills for their rebellion against Him (John 5:21).

The Father has made Him the judge of the living and the dead, committing all judgment to the Son, and has appointed that all should honor the Son just as they honor the Father (John 5:22-23).

God will judge the world through this man. The day for judgment is appointed, and He has been designated as the judge. "He has appointed a day in which He will judge the world in righteousness by that man" (Acts 17:31).

Therefore, we must all appear before the judgment seat of Christ, so that each person may receive what is due for the things done in the body, according to their actions. If they have accepted Him, they will receive heaven and salvation; if they have not, they will face hell and damnation.

For these reasons, He must be the judge:

1. Because of His humiliation. According to His Father's word, He humbled Himself and became obedient to death, even the death of the cross. "Therefore God also has highly exalted Him and given Him a name which is above every name: that at the name of Jesus every knee should bow, of those in heaven, and those on earth, and those under the earth; and that every tongue should confess that Jesus Christ is Lord, to the glory of God the Father."

This pertains to His role as judge and His authority to sit in judgment over angels and men (Philippians 2:7-11; Romans 14:10-11).

That all men might honor the Son just as they honor the Father. "For the Father judges no one, but has committed all judgment to the Son; that all men should honor the Son, even as they honor the Father" (John 5:22-23).

Because of His righteous judgment, this work is fit for no creature; it is only fit for the Son of God. For He will reward every man according to his ways (Revelation 22:12).

Because He is the Son of Man. He "has given Him authority to execute judgment also, because He is the Son of Man" (John 5:27).

12. Key Observations from the Text

Having briefly examined this text through explication, my next task is to address it through observation. I will also be brief in this, as the nature of the subject allows. "All that the Father gives Me shall come to Me; and him who comes to Me I will in no wise cast out" (John 6:37). Now I will present some observations and briefly discuss them before concluding the whole. The words explained provide us with several insights, including the following:

1. God the Father and Christ His Son are two distinct persons within the Godhead.

2. Together with the Holy Spirit, they have devised and determined the salvation of fallen mankind.

3. This plan is established as a covenant between these persons in the Godhead, which involves giving on the Father's part and receiving on the Son's. "All that the Father gives Me," etc.

4. Everyone that the Father has given to Christ, according to His will as expressed in the text, shall certainly come to Him.

5. Coming to Jesus Christ is not by the will, wisdom, or power of man, but by the gift, promise, and drawing of the Father. "All that the Father gives Me shall come."

6. Jesus Christ will be diligent in receiving those who come to Him and will not reject them. "And him who comes to Me I will in no wise cast out."

In addition to these points, there are other truths implied in the words:

7. Those who are coming to Jesus Christ often fear that He will not receive them.

8. Jesus Christ does not want those who are genuinely coming to Him to ever think that He will cast them out.

These observations are all contained within the words and are abundantly confirmed by the Scriptures of truth. However, I will not address all of them at this time. I will skip the first, second, third, fourth, and sixth observations, partly for the sake of brevity and partly because they have been touched upon in the explicatory part of the text.

I will therefore begin with the fifth observation, making it the first in order for the following discussion.

13. We Cannot Come Unless the Father Draws Us

First, coming to Christ is not by the will, wisdom, or power of man, but by the gift, promise, and drawing of the Father. This observation consists of two parts:

1. Coming to Christ is not by the will, wisdom, or power of man.

2. It is by the gift, promise, and drawing of the Father.

The text carries this truth within itself, as you will find if you refer back to the explanation of the first part. Therefore, I will follow the proposed method and show:

First, that coming to Christ is not by the will, wisdom, or power of man. This is true because the Word explicitly states that it is not.

It completely denies that it is by the will of man. "Not of blood, nor of the will of the flesh, nor of the will of man" (John 1:13). And again, "It is not of him who wills, nor of him who runs" (Romans 9:16).

It also denies that it is by the wisdom of man, as is evident from the following considerations:

In God's wisdom, it pleased Him that the world, through wisdom, should not know Him. If they cannot know Him by their wisdom, it follows that they cannot come to Him through that wisdom, for coming to Him occurs only after some knowledge of Him (1 Corinthians 1:21; Acts 13:27; Psalm 9:10).

The wisdom of man, in God's view, is regarded as foolishness. "Has not God made foolish the wisdom of this world?" (1 Corinthians 1:20). Furthermore, the wisdom of this world is foolishness with God (1:14). If God has made the wisdom of this world foolish, and if this wisdom is foolishness to Him, then it is unlikely that a sinner could become wise enough to come to Jesus Christ through it. This is especially true when you consider that the doctrine of a crucified Christ, and thus salvation through Him, is considered foolishness by the wisdom of the world. Therefore, it cannot be that a person would be drawn to come to Him through that wisdom (1 Corinthians 3:19; 1:18,23).

God considers the wisdom of this world to be one of His greatest enemies. Therefore, no one can come to Jesus Christ through that wisdom. It is unlikely that something God views as an enemy would lead a person to that which pleases Him most—coming to Christ.

This is evident because the wisdom of this world shows the greatest contempt for the work of His Son, as demonstrated by its belief that His crucifixion is foolishness. Yet, this crucifixion is one of the highest displays of Divine wisdom (Ephesians 1:7-8).

God has threatened to destroy this wisdom, to bring it to nothing, and to cause it to perish. Surely, He would not do this if it were not an enemy, especially if it could guide people to Jesus Christ (Isaiah 29:14; 1 Corinthians 1:19).

He has rejected this wisdom from assisting in the ministry of His Word, deeming it fruitless and ineffective (1 Corinthians 2:4, 6, 12, 13).

Moreover, it leads to the destruction of those who seek and pursue it (1 Corinthians 1:18, 19). God has proclaimed that if anyone wishes to be wise in this world, they must become a fool in the eyes of this world to gain true wisdom. "If anyone seems to be wise in this world, let him become a fool that he may be wise. For the wisdom of this world is foolishness with God" (1 Corinthians 3:18-20).

Coming to Christ is not by the power of man. This is evident from what has been previously stated. A person's power in this matter is either motivated by love or a sense of necessity. However, the wisdom of this world does not instill in a person either love for or a sense of need for Jesus Christ. Therefore, their power remains dormant in this regard.

What power does a person have who is spiritually dead, as every natural man is, being dead in trespasses and sins? Just as a person in a grave is dead to the things of this world, so too is the natural man dead to the things of God's New Testament. What power, then, does he have to come to Jesus Christ? (John 5:25; Ephesians 2:1; Colossians 2:13).

God forbids the mighty man from boasting in his strength, stating clearly, "By strength shall no man prevail." He also says, "Not by might, nor by power, but by My Spirit," says the Lord (Jeremiah 9:23-24; 1 Samuel 2:9; Zechariah 4:6; 1 Corinthians 1:27-31).

Paul acknowledges that even a converted man does not possess the power within himself to think a good thought. If he cannot do even the least of things, then no one can come to Jesus Christ by their own power (2 Corinthians 2:5).

Thus, we are said to be made willing to come by the power of God. We are raised from a state of sin to a state of grace by His power, and we believe—meaning we come—through the exceeding greatness of His mighty power (Psalm 110:3; Colossians 2:12; Ephesians 1:18, 20; Job 23:14). This would not be necessary if man had the power or will to come, or even the ability to think graciously about being willing to come to Jesus Christ on his own.

Next, I will provide proof for the second part of the observation, which states that coming to Christ is by the gift, promise, and drawing of the Father. This has already been addressed in the explicatory part of the text, to which I refer the reader. Here, I will present a couple more texts to support this point before moving on to the use and application.

It is explicitly stated, "No man can come to Me unless the Father who sent Me draws him" (John 6:44). This verse indicates not only a lack of power in man but also a lack of will to come to Jesus Christ. They must be drawn; they do not come unless they are drawn.

Notice that it is not man, nor all the angels in heaven, who can draw even one sinner to Jesus Christ. No one comes to Me unless the Father who sent Me draws him.

Furthermore, "No man can come to Me unless it has been granted to him by My Father" (John 6:65). It is a heavenly gift that enables a person to come to Jesus Christ.

Again, "It is written in the prophets, 'And they shall all be taught by God.' Therefore, everyone who has heard and learned from the Father comes to Me" (John 6:45).

I will not elaborate further, but I will make some use and application of this, and then proceed to the next observation.

Use and Application of Observation

First Use. Is it true? Is coming to Jesus Christ not by the will, wisdom, or power of man, but by the gift, promise, and drawing of the Father? Then those who emphasize the will, wisdom, and power of man as sufficient to bring people to Christ are to be blamed.

There are some individuals who believe they cannot be contradicted when they advocate for the will, wisdom, and power of man concerning matters of Christ's kingdom. However, I would say to such a person that they have yet to understand what the Scriptures teach about themselves. They do not truly know what it means to come to Christ through the teaching, gift, and drawing of the Father. Such a person has set up God's enemy in opposition to Him and continues in acts of defiance. The Scriptures also teach what their end will be without a new birth, but we will move on from this.

Second Use. Is it true? Is coming to Jesus Christ by the gift, promise, and drawing of the Father? Then let believers learn to attribute their coming to Christ to the gift, promise, and drawing of the Father. Christian, bless God, who has given you to Jesus Christ by promise;

and again, bless God for drawing you to Him. And why you? Why not someone else? Oh, that the glory of electing love should rest upon your head, and that the glory of God's exceeding grace should take hold of your heart and bring you to Jesus Christ!

Third Use. Is it true that coming to Jesus Christ is by the Father, as stated? Then this should teach us to hold those who are truly coming to Jesus Christ in high esteem. I say, we should have a high regard for them because of Him through whose grace they are made to come to Jesus Christ.

We see that when individuals, with the help of human abilities, achieve knowledge and accomplish things that, when done, are wonders to the world, the one who did it is esteemed and praised. Indeed, how their intellect, skills, industry, and tireless efforts are admired! Yet, this person, in this regard, is merely of the world, and their work is the result of natural ability. The things they attain ultimately lead to vanity and vexation of spirit. Furthermore, perhaps in pursuing these achievements, they sin against God, waste their time in vain pursuits, and ultimately lose their souls by neglecting better things; yet they are admired! But I say, if this person's talents, labor, diligence, and the like can earn them such applause and esteem in the world, how much more esteem should we have for one who, by the gift, promise, and power of God, is coming to Jesus Christ?

This is a person with whom God is present, in whom God works and walks; a person whose actions are governed and directed by the mighty hand of God and the effective working of His power. Here is a person!

This person, by the power of God's might, which works in them, is able to cast aside the entire world, along with all its lusts and pleasures, and to overcome all the challenges that men and devils can set against them. Here is a person!

This person is traveling to Mount Zion, the heavenly Jerusalem, the city of the living God, to an innumerable company of angels, to the spirits of just men made perfect, to God the Judge of all, and to Jesus. Here is a person!

This man can look upon death with comfort. He can laugh at destruction when it comes. He longs to hear the sound of the last trumpet and to see his Judge coming in the clouds of heaven. Here is a man indeed!

Let Christians, then, esteem each other as such. I know you do this; but do it more and more. To help you do this, consider these two or three things.

1. These are the objects of Christ's esteem (Matthew 12:48, 49; 15:22-28; Luke 7:9).

2. These are the objects of the esteem of angels (Daniel 9:12; 10:21, 22; 13:3, 4; Hebrews 2:14).

3. These have been the objects of the esteem of heathens when they were convinced about them (Daniel 5:10, 11; Acts 5:15; 1 Corinthians 14:24, 25).

"Let each of you esteem each other better than yourselves" (Philippians 2:2).

Use Four. Is it true that no man comes to Jesus Christ by the will, wisdom, and power of man, but by the gift, promise, and drawing of the Father? Then this shows us how horribly ignorant those are who make the man coming to Christ the object of their contempt and rage. These are unreasonable and wicked men; men in whom there is no faith (2 Thessalonians 3:2).

Sinners, if you only knew what a blessed thing it is to come to Jesus Christ, and that by the help and drawing of the Father, you would endure a thousand years in hell before you would turn your spirits against him that God is drawing to Jesus Christ, and also against the

God who draws him.

But, faithless sinner, let us consider this matter. What has this man done against you, that is coming to Jesus Christ? Why do you make him the object of your scorn? Does his coming to Jesus Christ offend you? Does his pursuit of his own salvation offend you? Does his forsaking of his sins and pleasures offend you?

Poor coming man! "Shall we sacrifice the abomination of the Egyptians before their eyes, and will they not stone us?" (Exodus 8:26).

But, I ask, why be offended at this? Is he any worse for coming to Jesus Christ, or for loving and serving Him? Is he any more foolish for fleeing from that which will drown you in hellfire, and for seeking eternal life?

Besides, consider this: he does this not of himself, but by the drawing of the Father. Come, let me tell you in your ear, you who will not come to Him yourself, and you who would hinder him — You shall be judged for hating, maligning, and reproaching Jesus Christ, to whom this poor sinner is coming.

You shall be judged for hating the Father, by whose powerful drawing this sinner comes.

You shall also be judged for doing despite to the Spirit of grace in him that is, by its help, coming to Jesus Christ. What do you say now? Will you stand by your actions? Will you continue to scorn and reproach the living God? Do you think you will fare well on the day of judgment? "Can your heart endure, or can your hands be strong, in the days that I shall deal with you?" says the Lord (Ezekiel 22:14; John 15:18-25; Jude 15; 1 Thessalonians 4:8).

Use Five. Is it true that no man comes to Jesus Christ by the will, wisdom, and power of man, but by the gift, promise, and drawing of the Father? Then this shows us how it comes to pass that weak means are so powerful as to bring men out of their sins to a heartfelt pursuit after Jesus Christ.

When God told Moses to speak to the people, He said, "I will give you counsel, and God shall be with you" (Exodus 18:19). When God speaks, when God works, who can stop it? No one! Then the work goes on!

Elijah threw his mantle upon the shoulders of Elisha, and what a wonderful work followed! When Jesus encountered the crowing of a cock, what work was there! Oh, when God is in the means, then that means, no matter how weak and contemptible in itself, will work wonders (1 Kings 19:19; Matthew 26:74, 75; Mark 14:71, 72; Luke 22:60-62).

The world did not understand, nor believe, that the walls of Jericho would fall at the sound of rams' horns; but when God decides to work, the means must be effective. A word spoken weakly, spoken with difficulty, in temptation, and amidst great contempt and scorn, works wonders if the Lord your God wills it to be so.

Is it true? Does no one come to Jesus Christ by the will, wisdom, and power of man, but by the gift, promise, and drawing of the Father? Then there is cause for Christians to stand in awe at the effective workings of God's providence, which He has used as means to bring them to Jesus Christ.

Although men are drawn to Christ by the power of the Father, that power is expressed through the use of means. These means vary; sometimes this, sometimes that. God is free to work through whatever means, at any time, and in any way He chooses. However, regardless of how insignificant or contemptible the means may appear, the God who commanded light to shine out of darkness, and who can make strength out of weakness, often uses very unlikely means to bring about the conversion and salvation of His people.

Therefore, you who have come to Christ—by means that seemed unlikely—pause, reflect, and marvel. In your wonder, magnify the almighty power that has made these means effective in bringing you to Jesus Christ.

What was the providence that God used as a means, either more remote or more immediate, to bring you to Jesus Christ? Was it a change of residence, a shift in your circumstances, the loss of loved ones, your possessions, or something similar? Was it your chance encounter with a good book, overhearing your neighbors discussing heavenly matters, witnessing God's judgments upon others, or your own deliverance from them? Or perhaps you found yourself unexpectedly under the ministry of a godly person?

Oh, take note of such providences! They were sent and orchestrated by mighty power to benefit you. God Himself has joined with this circumstance; indeed, He has blessed it so that it did not fail to accomplish the purpose for which He sent it.

God does not bless everyone with His providences in this way. How many thousands in this world go through the same experiences every day! Yet God is not working through those events to accomplish the same good for them as He has for your soul, by His effective workings. Oh, that Jesus Christ should meet you in this providence, in that dispensation, or through another ordinance! This is indeed grace! Therefore, it would be wise for you to marvel at this and to bless God for it.

Allow me to share some examples of those providences that have effectively brought salvation to the souls of His people.

The first example is that of the woman of Samaria. It was necessary for her to go out of the city to draw water, not before nor after, but precisely when Jesus Christ, her Savior, was arriving from afar and resting, weary, by the well. What a blessed providence this was! It was a providence orchestrated by almighty wisdom and power, leading to the conversion and salvation of this poor woman. Through this providence, she and her Savior were brought together so that the blessed work might be fulfilled upon her, according to the purpose determined by the Father (John 4).

What providence was it that there was a tree in the way for Zaccheus to climb, thereby giving Jesus the opportunity to call that chief of the publicans to Himself, even before he came down from the tree? (Luke 19).

Was it not also remarkable that the thief mentioned in the gospel was, by the providence of God, cast into prison to be condemned at the same session when Christ Himself was to die? Moreover, it happened that they were to be hanged together, allowing the thief to hear and observe Jesus in His last words, so that he might be converted before his death! (Luke 23).

What a strange providence it was, managed so uniquely by God, that Onesimus, when he ran away from his master, should be captured and, as I believe, thrown into that very prison where Paul was bound for the sake of the gospel. There, he might be converted by Paul and then sent back to his master, Philemon! Behold, "all things work together for good to those who love God, to those who are the called according to His purpose" (Romans 8:28).

Indeed, I have known individuals who were compelled to hear the Word preached against their will. Others attended not to listen, but to see and be seen, or even to mock and deride others. Some came merely to feast their eyes on beautiful sights. Yet God has used even these circumstances, including the wicked and sinful intentions of others, to bring them under the grace that might save their souls.

Does no one come to Jesus Christ except by the drawing of the Father? Then let me caution those poor sinners who are witnesses to the change that God has wrought in those coming to Jesus Christ. Do not attribute this work and change to other things and causes.

There are some poor sinners in the world who clearly see a change, a mighty change, in their neighbors and relatives who are coming to Jesus Christ. However, as I mentioned, they are ignorant and do not understand where this change comes from or where it goes, for "so is every one that is born of the Spirit" (John 3:8). Therefore, they attribute this change to other causes: such as melancholy, sitting alone, excessive reading, attending too many sermons, or overthinking what they hear.

On the other hand, they conclude that it is due to a lack of merry company or a lack of medicine. They advise these individuals to stop reading, attending sermons, and associating with sober people. Instead, they suggest they should be merry, gossip, and busy themselves with worldly matters, rather than sitting alone in contemplation.

But come, poor ignorant sinner, let me speak to you. It seems you have become a counselor for Satan. I tell you, you do not know what you are doing. Be careful not to spend your judgment in this way; you are judging foolishly and declaring to everyone who passes by that you are a fool. What? Do you consider convictions for sin, mourning for sin, and repentance for sin to be mere melancholy? This is akin to those who said, "These men are drunk with new wine" (Acts 2:13).

Poor ignorant sinner! Can you not judge better? Is sitting alone, pondering under God's hand, reading the Scriptures, and hearing sermons the way to be undone? May the Lord open your eyes and help you see your error! You have set yourself against God; you have despised the work of His hands and are attempting to harm souls. What? Can you offer no better counsel to those whom God has wounded than to send them to the ordinances of hell for help? You urge them to be merry and lighthearted, but do you not know that "the heart of fools is in the house of mirth?" (Eccl 7:4).

You advise them to avoid hearing powerful preachers, but is it not "better to hear the rebuke of the wise than for a man to hear the song of fools?" (Eccl 7:5). You encourage them to busy themselves with worldly matters, but do you not know that the Lord commands, "Seek first the kingdom of God and His righteousness?" (Matt 6:33).

Poor ignorant sinner! Listen to God's counsel and learn to be wiser. "Is any afflicted? Let him pray. Is any merry? Let him sing psalms" (James 5:13). "Blessed is the man who hears me" (Prov 8:32). And hear for the future, "Save yourselves from this untoward generation" (Acts 2:40). "Search the Scriptures" (John 5:39). "Give attention to reading" (1 Tim 4:13). "It is better to go to the house of mourning" (Eccl 7:2,3).

And will you judge him who does thus? Are you almost like Elymas the sorcerer, who sought to turn the deputy from the faith? You seek to pervert the right ways of the Lord. Take heed lest some heavy judgment overtake you (Acts 13:8-13).

What? Teach men to quench convictions? Lead them away from a serious consideration of the evil of sin, the terrors of the world to come, and how they shall escape the same? What? Teach men to put God and His Word out of their minds by running to merry company, to the world, or to gossip? This is as much as to bid them say to God, "Depart from us, for we desire not the knowledge of Your ways," or, "What is the Almighty that we should serve Him? Or what profit do we have if we keep His ways?" Here is a devil in disguise! What? Bid man walk "according to the course of this world, according to the prince of the power of the air, the spirit that now works in the children of disobedience" (Eph 2:2).

Two Objections Answered

Objection: But we do not know that such are coming to Jesus Christ; truly we wonder at them and think they are fools.

Answer: Do you not know that they are coming to Jesus Christ? They may be coming to Him, for all you know. Why will you be worse than a brute, speaking evil of things you do not understand? What? Are you made to be taken and destroyed? Must you utterly perish in your own corruptions? (2 Peter 2:12).

If you do not know them, let them be. If you cannot speak well of them, do not speak ill. "Refrain from these men, and let them alone; for if this counsel or this work be of men, it will come to nothing; but if it is of God, you cannot overthrow it, lest perhaps you be found even to fight against God" (Acts 5:38-39).

But why do you wonder at a work of conviction and conversion? Do you not know that this is the judgment of God upon you, "you despisers, behold and wonder, and perish?" (Acts 13:40-41). Why wonder and think they are fools? Is the way of the just an abomination to you? Consider this passage and be ashamed: "He who is upright in the way is an abomination to the wicked" (Prov 29:27). Your wonder at them indicates that you are strangers to yourselves, to conviction for sin, and to heartfelt desires to be saved, as well as to coming to Jesus Christ.

Objection: But how shall we know that such men are coming to Jesus Christ?

Answer: Who can make them see that Christ has made blind? (John 2:8-9). Nevertheless, because I endeavor your conviction, conversion, and salvation, consider:

Do they cry out against sin, burdened by it as if it were an exceedingly bitter thing? Do they flee from it as from the face of a deadly serpent? Do they lament the insufficiency of their own righteousness concerning justification in the sight of God? Do they cry out to the Lord Jesus to save them?

Do they see more worth and merit in one drop of Christ's blood to save them than in all the sins of the world to condemn them? Are they sensitive to sinning against Jesus Christ? Is His name, person, and work more precious to them than the glory of the world? Is this Word dear to them? Is faith in Christ, of which they are convinced by God's Spirit that they lack, precious to them?

Do they savor Christ in His Word, and do they leave all the world for His sake? Are they willing, with God's help, to take risks for His name, out of love for Him? Are His saints precious to them? If these things are true, whether you see them or not, these men are coming to Jesus Christ.

Psalm 51:7, 8; 1 Peter 1:18, 19; Romans 7:24; 2 Corinthians 5:2; Acts 5:41; James 2:7;

Song of Solomon 5:10-16; Psalm 119; John 13:35; 1 John 4:7; 3:14; John 16:9; Romans 14:23; Hebrews 11:6; Psalm 19:10, 11; Jeremiah 15:16; Hebrews 11:24-27; Acts 20:22-24;

21:13; Titus 3:15; 2 John 1; Ephesians 4:16; Philemon 7; 1 Corinthians 16:24.

14. Many Who Come to Christ Fear He Won't Accept Them

I come now to the second observation proposed to be discussed: that those who are coming to Jesus Christ are often heartily afraid that Jesus Christ will not receive them.

I mentioned that this observation is implied in the text. I gather this first from the broadness and openness of the promise: "I will in no wise cast out." If there were not a tendency within us to fear being cast out, Christ would not have needed to address our fears with such a strong and unique expression, "In no wise;" "And him that comes to me I will in no wise cast out."

There would be no need for such a promise to be crafted by the wisdom of heaven, worded in a way meant to shatter all objections of coming sinners, if they were not inclined to entertain such objections that discourage their souls. The phrase "in no wise" cuts the throat of all objections, and it was spoken by the Lord Jesus for that very purpose—to bolster the faith that is mixed with unbelief. It is, in essence, the summary of all promises; no objection regarding your unworthiness can be made that this promise will not resolve.

"But I am a great sinner," you say. "I will in no wise cast out," says Christ.

"But I am an old sinner," you say. "I will in no wise cast out," says Christ.

"But I am a hard-hearted sinner," you say. "I will in no wise cast out," says Christ.

"But I am a backsliding sinner," you say. "I will in no wise cast out," says Christ.

"But I have served Satan all my days," you say. "I will in no wise cast out," says Christ.

"But I have sinned against light," you say. "I will in no wise cast out," says Christ.

"But I have sinned against mercy," you say. "I will in no wise cast out," says Christ.

"But I have no good thing to bring with me," you say. "I will in no wise cast out," says Christ.

Thus, I could continue to the end of things, showing you that this promise was provided to answer all objections, and indeed does answer them. However, I ask, what need would there be for such a promise if those who are coming to Jesus Christ are not sometimes, indeed often, heartily afraid that "Jesus Christ will cast them out?"

Second, I will now provide two examples that seem to support the truth of this observation.

In Matthew 9:2, we read of a man who was paralyzed, coming to Jesus Christ, carried on a bed by his friends. He was coming for a reason that his friends were not aware of; he sought the pardon of his sins and the salvation of his soul. As soon as he entered the presence of Christ, Jesus told him, "Be of good cheer." This indicates that his heart was fainting.

But what was the cause of his faintness? Not his physical ailment, for which his friends had brought him to Christ, but rather the guilt and burden of his sins, for which he himself had come. Therefore, Jesus continued, "Be of good cheer, your sins are forgiven you."

Christ perceived that he was sinking in his mind regarding the fate of his most noble part, and thus He first addressed him concerning that. While his friends had enough faith for the healing of his body, he had little faith regarding the healing of his soul. Therefore, Christ lifted him up, saying, "Son, be of good cheer, your sins are forgiven you."

The story of the Prodigal Son is also relevant to this matter: "When he came to himself, he said, 'How many of my father's hired servants have bread enough and to spare, and I perish with hunger! I will arise and go to my father.'" This was a heartfelt declaration; but how did he fulfill his promise? I suspect not as well as he intended.

My reasoning is that as soon as he approached his father, the father fell upon his neck and kissed him, suggesting that the Prodigal was likely feeling dejected. The father's kiss served to remove doubts and fears. This is evident in the stories of Laban and Esau kissing Jacob, Joseph kissing his brothers, and David kissing Absalom (Genesis 31:55; 33:1-4; 48:9, 10; 2 Samuel 14:33).

Indeed, at first, he spoke sincerely, as many sinners do when they begin to come to Jesus Christ. Yet, it is likely that he had many thoughts between his initial step and the final one that brought him home. He may have wondered whether his father would receive him.

He might have thought, "I said I would go to my Father. But what if, when I arrive, he asks me where I have been all this time? What should I say then? If he asks me what happened to the portion of goods he gave me, what will I respond? If he inquires about my companions, what will I say? If he asks about my situation during my absence, what shall I say? And if he questions why I did not return sooner, what will I say?"

Thus, he might reason with himself, and being aware that he could only provide poor answers to any of these questions, it is no wonder he stood in need of a kiss from his father's lips. For had he answered truthfully, he would have had to admit, "I have been a frequenter of taverns and alehouses; I squandered my portion on riotous living; my companions were harlots; my highest achievement was becoming a swineherd; and had I been able to stay away any longer, I would not be here now seeking mercy."

Considering these things, and reflecting on how prone a poor man is to give way to despondency and doubt when truly awakened, it is no wonder that he may sink in his mind between the time of his first setting out and the moment he comes to his Father.

Thirdly, I believe that the agreement of all the saints in heaven confirms this truth: those who are coming to Jesus Christ are often genuinely afraid that He will not receive them.

Question: But what could be the reason for this fear? I will answer this question as follows:

It is not due to a lack of the revealed will of God, which provides sufficient grounds for the opposite belief. Indeed, the text itself lays a solid foundation for encouragement for those coming to Jesus Christ: "And him that cometh to me I will in no wise cast out."

It is not because there is a lack of invitations to come, for those are clear and abundant: "Come unto me, all ye that labor and are heavy laden, and I will give you rest" (Matt 11:28).

Neither is it due to a lack of evidence of Christ's willingness to receive, as the aforementioned texts and those that follow declare: "If any man thirst, let him come unto me, and drink" (John 7:37).

It is not because there are insufficient great and precious promises for those who come: "Wherefore come out from among them, and be ye separate, saith the Lord, and touch not the unclean thing, and I will receive you, and will be a Father unto you, and ye shall be my sons and daughters, saith the Lord Almighty" (2 Cor 6:17, 18).

It is not for lack of solemn oaths and commitments to save those who come: "For—because He could swear by no greater, He swore by Himself—that by two immutable things, in which it was impossible for God to lie, we might have a strong consolation, who have fled for refuge to lay hold upon the hope set before us" (Heb 6:13-18).

Neither is it due to a lack of great examples of God's mercy towards those who have come to Jesus Christ, which we read about abundantly in the Word. Therefore, we must conclude that the issue lies in what follows.

What prevents coming to Christ? First, it is a lack of knowledge of Christ. You know very little of the grace and kindness in the heart of Christ; you know very little of the virtue and merit of His blood; you know very little of His willingness to save you. This ignorance is the source of the fear that arises in your heart and causes you to doubt that Christ will receive you. Unbelief is the daughter of ignorance. Therefore, Christ says, "O fools, and slow of heart to believe" (Luke 24:25).

Slowness of heart to believe comes from foolishness regarding the things of Christ. This is evident to all who are aware of themselves and are seeking after Jesus Christ. The more ignorance there is, the more unbelief there is. The more knowledge of Christ one has, the more faith one possesses. "They that know Thy name will put their trust in Thee" (Psalm 9:10).

Therefore, the one who has just begun to come to Christ and has little knowledge of Him fears that Christ will not receive him. But the one who has been acquainted with Him longer "is strong and has overcome the wicked one" (1 John 2:13).

When Joseph's brothers came into Egypt to buy corn, it is said, "Joseph knew his brothers, but his brothers did not know him." What follows? Great mistrust of heart regarding their well-being, especially if Joseph answered them roughly, calling them spies and questioning their truthfulness.

Observe that as long as their ignorance about their brother persisted, whatever Joseph did was interpreted negatively. For instance, when Joseph instructed the steward of his house to bring them home to dine with him, how did they respond? They were afraid. "And the men were afraid because they were brought to Joseph's house." They said, "He seeks occasion against us, and will fall upon us, and take us for bondmen, and our asses" (Genesis 42:43).

What! Afraid to go to Joseph's house? He was their brother; he intended to feast them! But they were ignorant of his identity. As long as their ignorance lasted, their fear tormented them. Just like this, the sinner who has recently begun to come to Jesus Christ is unaware of the love and compassion that Christ has for those who come to Him. Therefore, he doubts, fears, and feels uncertain in his heart.

Coming sinner, Christ invites you to dine and sup with Him. He invites you to a banquet of wine, to come into His wine cellar, and His banner over you shall be love (Revelation 3:20; Song of Solomon 2:5).

But the sinner responds, "I doubt it." Yet, it is answered that He calls you, inviting you to His banquet, to His flagons and apples, to His wine and to the juice of His pomegranate. "O, I fear, I doubt, I mistrust; I tremble in expectation of the contrary!"

Come out of the man, you cowardly ignorance! Do not be afraid, sinner; only believe. "He that comes to Christ, He will in no wise cast out."

Let the coming sinner, therefore, seek after more knowledge of Jesus Christ. Pursue it as silver, and dig for it as for hidden treasure. This will embolden you; this will make you grow stronger and stronger.

"I know whom I have believed," said Paul; and what follows? "And I am persuaded that He is able to keep that which I have committed to Him against that day" (2 Timothy 1:12).

What had Paul committed to Jesus Christ? The answer is, he had committed his soul to Him. But why did he commit his soul to Him? Because he knew Him. He knew Him to be faithful and kind. He knew that He would not fail him nor forsake him; therefore, he laid his soul down at His feet and committed it to Him to keep against that day.

Secondly, your fears that Christ will not receive you may also arise from your earnest and strong desires for salvation through Him. Strong desires to have are often accompanied by strong fears of missing out.

For example, the ruler of the synagogue had a great desire for his daughter to live, and that desire was accompanied by fear that she would not. Therefore, Christ said to him, "Be not afraid" (Mark 5:36).

Suppose a young man has his heart set on a virgin to marry her. If he fears he will not obtain her, it is when he begins to love her. He thinks that someone might come between him and his love; they might find fault with his person, his estate, his conditions, or something else.

Thoughts begin to work: "She does not like me," or something similar. This is how it is with the soul at first coming to Jesus Christ. You love Him, and your love produces jealousy, which often gives rise to fears.

Now you fear the sins of your youth, the sins of your old age, the sins of your calling, the sins of your Christian duties, the sins of your heart, or something else. You think that something will alienate the heart and affections of Jesus Christ from you. You believe He sees something in you for which He will refuse your soul.

But be content; a little more knowledge of Him will help you take heart. Your earnest desires will not be accompanied by such burning fears. You will later say, "This is my infirmity" (Psalm 77:10).

You are sick with love, a very sweet disease, yet every disease has some weakness accompanying it. I wish this condition, if it can be called so, were more widespread. I would gladly die of this disease; it is better than life itself, even though it comes with fears.

But you cry, "I cannot obtain." Well, do not be too hasty in making conclusions. If Jesus Christ had not put His finger in at the hole of the lock, your heart would not be troubled for Him (Song of Solomon 5:4).

Mark how the prophet puts it: "They shall walk after the Lord; He shall roar like a lion; when He roars, then the children shall tremble from the west; they shall tremble like a bird out of Egypt, and like a dove out of the land of Assyria" (Hosea 11:10-11).

When God roars (as often the coming soul hears Him roar), what man that is coming can do otherwise than tremble? (Amos 3:8). But trembling, he comes: "He sprang in, and came trembling, and fell down before Paul and Silas" (Acts 16:29).

If you were to ask the young man we mentioned earlier, "How long have you feared that you might miss the damsel you love?" he would answer, "Ever since I began to love her."

But did you not fear it before? "No, nor should I fear it now, but for my intense love for her."

Come, sinner, let us apply this: "How long have you feared that Jesus Christ will not receive you?" Your answer is, "Ever since I began to desire that He would save my soul."

You began to fear when you began to come, and the more your heart burns with desires for Him, the more you feel your heart fear that you shall not be saved by Him.

See now, did I not tell you that your fears are merely the consequence of strong desires? Well, fear not, coming sinner; thousands of coming souls are in your condition, and yet they will safely find their way into Christ's bosom. "Say," says Christ, "to those who are of a fearful heart, Be strong, fear not; your God will come and save you" (Isaiah 35:4; 63:1).

Third, your fear that Christ will not receive you may arise from a sense of your own unworthiness. You see what a poor, wretched, worthless creature you are; and seeing this, you fear that Christ will not receive you.

Alas, you say, "I am the vilest of all men; a town-sinner, a ringleader in sin! I am not only a sinner myself, but I have made others twofold worse, the children of hell as well.

Besides, now that I am under some awakenings and stirrings of mind after salvation, I find my heart rebellious, carnal, hard, treacherous, desperate, prone to unbelief and despair. It forgets the Word; it wanders; it runs to the ends of the earth.

I am convinced that there is not one in all the world who has such a desperate wicked heart as mine. My soul is careless to do good, but none more earnest to do that which is evil.

Can someone like me live in glory? Can a holy, just, and righteous God even consider saving such a vile creature as I? I fear it. Will He show wonders to such a dead dog as I? I doubt it.

I feel cast out, loathed by myself; I stink in my own nostrils. How can I then be accepted by a holy and sin-abhorring God? (Psalm 38:5-7; Ezekiel 11:20-42, 44).

I would be saved; and who would not, were they in my condition? Indeed, I marvel at the madness and folly of others when I see them carelessly leaping around the mouth of hell!

Bold sinner, how dare you tempt God by laughing at the breach of His holy law? But alas! They are not so bad in one way, yet I am worse in another: I wish I were anyone but myself; and yet, here again, I do not know what to wish.

When I see those whom I believe are coming to Jesus Christ, I bless them! But I am confounded in myself, seeing how unlike I think I am to every good man in the world. They can read, hear, pray, remember, repent, be humble, and do everything better than this vile wretch.

I, a vile wretch, am good for nothing but to burn in hellfire, and when I think of that, I am confounded too!

The sense of unworthiness creates and heightens fears in the hearts of those who are coming to Jesus Christ; but it should not. Who needs the physician but the sick? Or who did Christ come into the world to save but the chief of sinners? (Mark 2:17; 1 Timothy 1:15).

Therefore, the more you see your sins, the faster you should flee to Jesus Christ. Let the awareness of your own unworthiness drive you to Him even more quickly.

Consider the man who carries his broken arm in a sling to the bone-setter. As he thinks of his broken arm and feels the pain and anguish, he hastens his pace to the healer.

If Satan meets you and asks, "Where are you going?" tell him you are wounded and are going to the Lord Jesus. If he objects by pointing out your unworthiness, respond by saying that just as the sick seek the physician, and just as one with broken bones seeks the one who can set them, you are going to Jesus Christ for healing for your sin-sick soul.

But often, when someone is fleeing for their life, they despair of escaping and thus surrender themselves to the pursuer.

But rise up, sinner; be of good cheer! Christ came to save the unworthy. Do not be faithless, but believe. Come away, for the Lord Jesus calls you, saying, "And him that comes to me I will in no wise cast out."

Fourth, your fear that Christ will not receive you may come from a sense of the immense mercy involved in being saved. Sometimes, salvation appears so great, so wonderful, that the very thought of its excellence can lead to unbelief in the hearts of those who sincerely desire it. As David said, "Does it seem like a small thing to you to be a king's son-in-law?" (1 Samuel 18:23). The thoughts of the greatness and glory of what is offered—such as heaven, eternal life, and eternal glory, to be with God, Christ, and angels—can feel overwhelming. These are magnificent things, too good for someone who sees themselves as small and insignificant, too rich for someone who is truly poor in spirit.

Moreover, the Holy Spirit has a way of magnifying heavenly things in the understanding of the sinner who is coming to Christ. At the same time, He also magnifies the sin and unworthiness of that sinner. The soul wonders in amazement, saying, "What! To be made like angels, like Christ, to live in eternal bliss, joy, and happiness! This is for angels and for those who can walk like angels!"

Imagine if a prince, a duke, or an earl sent a servant to invite a poor, shabby beggar to be his wife. The servant would say, "My lord has sent me to take you to him as his wife. He is rich, beautiful, and possesses excellent qualities; he is loving, meek, humble, well-spoken," and so on. What would this poor, shabby creature think? What could she say? How would she respond? When King David sent for Abigail, even though she was a wealthy woman, she said, "Here is your servant, let her be a servant to wash the feet of the servants of my lord" (1 Samuel 25:40-41). She was overwhelmed and could hardly find the words to express herself because the offer was so great, far beyond what could reasonably be expected.

But suppose this great person were to pursue his proposal and send for this poor creature again. What would she say now? Would she not think, "You must be mocking me"? But what if he insisted that he was serious and that his lord truly wanted her as his wife? Suppose he managed to convince her to believe his message and prepare for her journey. Yet, every thought of her humble background would leave her feeling confused. Her lack of beauty would make her feel ashamed, and just the thought of being embraced by him would fill her with trembling. She would call herself a fool for believing the messenger and might decide not to go. If she thought of being bold, she would blush, and the mere idea of being rejected when she finally approached him would make her feel as if she might faint.

Is it any wonder, then, that a soul overwhelmed by the sense of glory and its own insignificance feels confused and fears that the glory it longs for is too great, too good, and too rich for someone like them? The thought of heaven and eternal glory is so vast, and I, who desire it, feel so small and insignificant that the very idea of obtaining it leaves me in a state of confusion.

Thus, I say, the greatness of what is desired can completely overwhelm the mind of the one desiring it. "Oh, it is too big! It is too great a mercy!" But, coming sinner, let me reason with you. You say it is too big, too great. Well, will anything less satisfy your soul? Will anything less than heaven, glory, and eternal life fulfill your desires? No, nothing less will do; yet I fear they are too big and too good for me to ever obtain.

Well, as big and as good as they are, God gives them to those like you; they are not too big for God to give—no, not too big to give freely. Be content; let God give as He truly is; He is the eternal God and gives like Himself. When kings give, they do not give as poor men do. It is said that Nabal made a feast in his house like a king's feast, and again, "All these things did Araunah, as a king, give to David" (1 Samuel 25:36; 2 Samuel 24:23). Now, God is a great king; let Him give like a king; indeed, let Him give like Himself, and you receive like yourself. He has all, and you have nothing. God told His people of old that He would save them in truth and righteousness and that they would return to and enjoy the land, which had previously cast them out due to their sins. He added, "If it is marvelous in the eyes of the remnant of this people in these days, should it also be marvelous in My eyes?" says the Lord of hosts (Zechariah 8:6).

As if to say, they are now in captivity and feel small in their own eyes; therefore, they think the mercy of returning to Canaan is too wonderfully great for them to enjoy. But if it seems so in their eyes, it is not so in Mine; I will act for them as God, if they will only receive My bounty like sinners. Coming sinner, God can give you His heavenly

Canaan and the glory of it; indeed, no one has ever received it except as a gift, a free gift. He has given us His Son, "How shall He not with Him also freely give us all things?" (Romans 8:32).

It was not the worthiness of Abraham, Moses, David, Peter, or Paul that made them inheritors of heaven, but the mercy of God. If God considers you worthy, do not judge yourself unworthy; instead, accept it and be thankful. It is a good sign that He intends to give to you if He has stirred your heart to ask. "Lord, You have heard the desire of the humble; You will prepare their heart; You will cause Your ear to hear" (Psalm 10:17).

When God is said to incline His ear, it implies an intention to bestow the mercy desired. Therefore, take it; your wisdom will be to receive, not to hesitate due to your own unworthiness. It is said, "He raises the poor out of the dust and lifts the beggar from the dunghill to set them among princes and to make them inherit the throne of glory." Again, "He raises the poor out of the dust and lifts the needy out of the dunghill, that He may set him with princes, even with the princes of His people" (1 Samuel 2:8; Psalm 113:7-8). You can also see that when God made a wedding feast for His Son, He did not invite the great, the rich, or the mighty, but the poor, the maimed, the lame, and the blind (Matthew 12; Luke 14).

Fifth, your fears that Christ will not receive you may arise from the terrifying roar of the devil, who pursues you. Anyone who hears him roar must be a mighty Christian if they can deliver themselves from fear at that moment. He is referred to as a roaring lion. To allude to Isaiah, "If one looks into them, they have darkness and sorrow, and the light is darkened in the heavens thereof" (1 Peter 5:8; Isaiah 5:30).

There are two objections that Satan uses to frighten those who are coming to Jesus Christ.

1. That they are not elected.

2. That they have committed the sin against the Holy Spirit.

To both of these, I will respond briefly. Regarding election, from which you fear you are excluded, the text itself provides you with help against this doubt, and that by a double argument.

Coming to Christ is made possible by the gift, promise, and drawing of the Father. If you are coming, then God has given you this gift, promised it to you, and is drawing you to Jesus Christ. Coming sinner, hold on to this truth. When Satan begins to roar again, respond by saying, "But I feel my heart moving toward Jesus Christ." This desire would not be present if it were not given to me by promise and drawn by the power of the Father.

Jesus Christ has promised, "Him who comes to Me I will in no wise cast out." If He has said it, will He not fulfill it, including your salvation? As I have mentioned before, not casting out means receiving and admitting you to the benefits of salvation. If the Father has given you this gift, as is evident by your coming, and if Christ will receive you — because He has said, "I will in no wise cast out" — then be confident. Let those conclusions, which flow as naturally from the text as light from the sun or water from a fountain, support you.

If Satan objects, saying, "But you are not elected," respond, "But I am coming, Satan; I am coming." I could not be coming unless the Father were drawing me. I am coming to a Lord Jesus who will in no wise cast me out. Furthermore, Satan, if I were not elect, the Father would not draw me, nor would the Son graciously open His arms to me. I am convinced that none of the non-elect will ever be able to say, not even on the day of judgment, "I sincerely came to Jesus Christ." They may come feignedly, as Judas and Simon Magus did, but that is not our concern. Therefore, O honest-hearted coming sinner, do not be afraid, but come.

Regarding the second part of the objection about committing the sin against the Holy Spirit, the same argument refutes that as well. I will argue as follows:

Coming to Christ is a special gift from the Father; however, the Father does not give such a gift to those who have committed that sin. Therefore, if you are coming, you have not committed that sin. It is evident that the Father does not give such a gift to those who have sinned that sin because such individuals have sinned themselves out of God's favor. "They shall never have forgiveness" (Matthew 12:32). It is a special favor of God to enable a person to come to Jesus Christ, as this grants them forgiveness. Therefore, he who comes has not committed that sin.

Moreover, those who have sinned the sin against the Holy Spirit have excluded themselves from an interest in the sacrifice of Christ's body and blood. "There remains no more sacrifice for sins" (Hebrews 10:26). God does not grant grace to any of them to come to Christ, as they have no share in the sacrifice of His body and blood. Therefore, if you are coming to Him, you have not committed that sin.

Coming to Christ is by the special drawing of the Father. "No one can come to Me unless the Father who sent Me draws him" (John 6:44). However, the Father does not draw to Christ those for whom He has not allotted forgiveness through His blood. Therefore, those who are coming to Jesus Christ have not committed that sin, because He has allotted them forgiveness through His blood. It is clear that the Father cannot draw those to Jesus Christ for whom He has not allotted forgiveness of sins, as that would be a mockery, unworthy of His wisdom, justice, holiness, or goodness.

Coming to Jesus Christ places a person under the promise of forgiveness and salvation. However, it is impossible for someone who has sinned that sin to ever be placed under such a promise. Therefore, anyone who has committed that sin can never have the heart to come to Jesus Christ.

Coming to Jesus Christ places a person under His intercession. "For He ever lives to make intercession for them that come" (Hebrews 7:25).

Therefore, anyone coming to Jesus Christ cannot have sinned that sin. Christ has forbidden His people to pray for those who have committed that sin, and thus He will not pray for them Himself; He prays for those who come.

Anyone who has committed that sin regards Christ as having no more value than a dead man. "For he has crucified to himself the Son of God" and has counted His precious blood as the blood of something unholy (Hebrews 6:6).

A person who holds such a low opinion of Christ will never come to Him for life. In contrast, the one who comes to Christ has a high regard for His person, blood, and merits. Therefore, it is clear that anyone who is coming has not committed that sin.

If someone who has committed that sin could still come to Jesus Christ, then the truth of God would be overturned. For it says in one place, "He shall never have forgiveness," and in another, "I will in no wise cast him out." Therefore, since he may never have forgiveness, he will never have the heart to come to Jesus Christ. It is impossible for such a person to be renewed, either to or by repentance (Hebrews 6). Therefore, do not trouble your head or heart about this matter; he who comes to Jesus Christ cannot have sinned against the Holy Spirit.

Sixth, your fears that Christ will not receive you may arise from your own folly in trying to dictate to God a specific way to bring you to Jesus Christ. Some souls that are coming to Jesus Christ are great tormentors of themselves on this account. They conclude that if their coming to Jesus Christ is genuine, they must be brought home in a certain manner.

For example:

1. One might say, "If God is bringing me to Jesus Christ, then He will load me with the guilt of sin until I am in agony."

2. Another might think, "If God is indeed bringing me home to Jesus

Christ, then I must be assaulted with dreadful temptations from the devil."

3. Yet another might believe, "If God is truly bringing me to Jesus Christ, then even when I approach Him, I shall have wonderful revelations of Him."

This is the way that some sinners prescribe for God; however, He may not follow their prescribed path. Yet, He will still bring them to Jesus Christ. Because they do not come by the way they have outlined, they find themselves at a loss. They expect a heavy load and burden, but perhaps God gives them a glimpse of their lost condition without adding that heavy weight. They anticipate fearful temptations from Satan, but God knows they are not yet ready for them, nor is the time right for Him to be honored in such a condition. They look for great and glorious revelations of Christ, grace, and mercy, but perhaps God simply removes the yoke from their jaws and lays food before them.

And so, they find themselves at a loss while still coming to Jesus Christ. "I drew them," says God, "with cords of a man, with bands of love. I took the yoke from off their jaws and laid meat before them" (Hosea 11:4).

Now, I say, if God brings you to Christ, and not by the way you have appointed, then you are at a loss; and for your being at a loss, you may thank yourself. God has more ways than you know to bring a sinner to Jesus Christ, but He will not give you an account in advance of which way He will use (Isaiah 40:13; Job 33:13). Sometimes He has His ways in the whirlwind; yet at other times, the Lord is not there (Nahum 1:3; 1 Kings 19:11). If God chooses to deal more gently with you than with others of His children, do not begrudge it. Do not refuse the waters that flow gently, lest He bring upon you the waters of the rivers, strong and many, even these two smoking firebrands: the devil and the guilt of sin (Isaiah 8:6,7). He says to Peter, "Follow Me." And what thunder did Zacchaeus hear or see? Christ said, "Come down," and Luke tells us, "he came down and received Him joyfully."

But had Peter or Zacchaeus made the objections you have made and directed the Spirit of the Lord as you have done, they might have waited a long time before finding themselves coming to Jesus Christ. Furthermore, I will tell you that the great sense of sin, the terrifying roar of the devil, and an abundance of revelations will not prove that God is bringing your soul to Jesus Christ, as Balaam, Cain, Judas, and others can testify.

Moreover, consider that what you do not experience now, you may encounter at another time, and that could lead to your distraction. Therefore, instead of being discontent because you are not in the fire, or because you do not hear the sound of the trumpet and the alarm of war, "Pray that you enter not into temptation." Yes, come boldly to the throne of grace to obtain mercy and find grace to help in your time of need (Psalm 88:15; Matthew 26:41; Hebrews 4:16).

Poor creature! You cry out, "If I were tempted, I could come faster and with more confidence to Christ." You say you do not know what to do. What does Job say? "Withdraw Your hand far from me, and let not Your dread make me afraid. Then call, and I will answer; or let me speak, and You answer me" (Job 13:21,22). It is not the overwhelming load of sin, but the discovery of mercy; not the roaring of the devil, but the drawing of the Father that makes a person come to Jesus Christ. I know this from experience.

True, sometimes, indeed most often, those who come to Jesus Christ do so in the way you desire: the burdened, tempted way. However, the Lord also leads some by the waters of comfort. If I were to choose when to embark on a long journey, whether in the dead of winter or in pleasant spring, I would choose to undertake it in the spring, even if it were a very profitable journey, such as coming to Christ.

But I say, if I could choose the time, I would prefer to go in the pleasant spring, because the way would be more delightful, the days longer and warmer, and the nights shorter and not so cold. It is noteworthy that the very argument you use to weaken your resolve in the journey is the same argument Christ Jesus uses to encourage His beloved to come to Him: "Rise up," says He, "my love, my fair one, and come away." Why? "For behold, the winter is past, the rain is over and gone; the flowers appear on the earth, the time of the singing of birds has come, and the voice of the turtle is heard in our land; the fig tree puts forth her green figs, and the vines with the tender grape give a good smell. Arise, my love, my fair one, and come away" (Song of Solomon 2:10-13).

Do not trouble yourself, coming sinner. If you see your lost condition due to original and actual sin; if you recognize your need for the spotless righteousness of Jesus Christ; if you are willing to be found in Him and to take up your cross and follow Him, then pray for a fair wind and good weather, and come away. Do not linger in doubt and uncertainty, but come away to Jesus Christ. I urge you to do this, lest you tempt God to lay the sorrows of a travailing woman upon you. Your folly in this matter may provoke Him to do so. Remember what follows: "The sorrows of a travailing woman shall come upon him." Why? "He is an unwise son; for he should not stay long in the place of the breaking forth of children" (Hosea 13:13).

Seventh, your fears that Christ will not receive you may arise from the shortcomings you find in your soul, even while you are coming to Him. Some, even as they are approaching Jesus Christ, find themselves growing worse and worse; and this is indeed a severe trial for the poor coming sinner.

15. Fear of Not Coming to Christ Fast Enough

To explain myself, there is a person coming to Jesus Christ who, when he first began to seek Him, was sensitive, affectionate, and broken in spirit. However, now he has grown dark, insensible, hard-hearted, and inclined to neglect spiritual duties, among other things.

Furthermore, he now finds within himself inclinations toward unbelief, atheism, blasphemy, and similar thoughts. He feels that he cannot tremble at God's Word, His judgment, or even at the thought of hellfire. He believes he cannot be sorry for these things. This is indeed a sad situation.

The man under the sixth head complains of a lack of temptations, but you have enough of them. Are you glad for them, tempted, coming sinner? Those who have never been exercised by such trials may think it is a fine thing to be within their range. However, the one who is there is ready to sweat blood from the sorrow of his heart and to howl from the vexation of his spirit!

This man is in the wilderness among wild beasts. Here he sees a bear, there a lion, yonder a leopard, a wolf, a dragon; devils of all sorts, doubts of all sorts, fears of all sorts, haunt and torment his soul. He sees smoke and even feels fire and brimstone scattered upon his secret places. He hears the sound of a horrible tempest.

Oh, my friends, even the Lord Jesus, who knew all things, found no pleasure in temptations, nor did He desire to be with them. Therefore, one text says, "He was led," and another, "He was driven," by the Spirit into the wilderness to be tempted by the devil (Matthew 4:1; Mark 1:12).

But to return. Thus it sometimes happens to those who are coming to Jesus Christ. It is indeed a sad occurrence! One would think that someone fleeing from impending wrath has little need of such burdens. Yet it is so, and woeful experience proves it. The church of old complained that her enemies overtook her in the straits, just between hope and fear, heaven and hell (Lamentations 1).

This person feels the weakness of their flesh; they find within themselves a tendency toward despair. Now, they argue with God, flinging themselves about like a wild bull in a net, and the guilt of all their actions returns upon them, crushing them to pieces. Yet they feel their heart is so hard that they believe they cannot find any kind of relief from their failings. They are a mass of confusion in their own eyes, with a spirit and actions that are without order.

Temptations serve the Christian as a shepherd's dog serves the foolish sheep. The dog comes behind the flock, runs upon it, pulls it down, worries it, wounds it, and grievously soils it with dirt and wet in the lowest places of the field, not leaving it until it is half dead. And even then, it does not stop unless God rebukes it.

Now there is room for fears of being cast away. The sinner says, "Now I see I am lost." They think, "This is not coming to Jesus Christ; a desperate, hard, and wretched heart like mine cannot be a gracious one." When told to be better, they reply, "I cannot; no, I cannot."

Why temptations assail God's people

Question: But what will you say to a soul in this condition?

Answer: I will say that temptations have attended the best of God's people. I will say that temptations come to do us good; and I will also say that there is a difference between growing worse and worse and seeing more clearly how bad you truly are.

There is a man of an ill-favored countenance who has too high a conceit of his beauty. Lacking the benefit of a mirror, he continues to stand in his own conceit. Eventually, a painter is sent to him, who accurately depicts his unattractive face. Upon seeing it, he begins to realize that he is not nearly as handsome as he thought.

Coming sinner, your temptations are like these painters; they have revealed your ill-favored heart and set it before your eyes, so now you see how unappealing you truly are. Hezekiah was a good man, yet when he lay sick, he may have had too good an opinion of his heart. It is possible that the Lord, upon his recovery, allowed him to face a temptation so that he might better understand all that was in his heart. Compare Isaiah 38:1-3 with 2 Chronicles 32:31.

Alas! We are exceedingly sinful, but we do not see it fully until a time of temptation comes. When it does, it acts like a painter, revealing our heart in its true state. Yet the sight of what we are should not keep us from coming to Jesus Christ.

There are two ways by which God allows a person to see the wickedness of their heart: one is through the light of the Word and Spirit of God, and the other is through the temptations of the devil. By the first, we see our wickedness in one way; by the second, in another. Through the light of the Word and Spirit of God, you gain insight into your wickedness, just as the light of the sun reveals the spots and stains in your house or clothing. This light shows you the need for cleansing but does not make the blemishes appear more abominable. However, when Satan comes and tempts, he infuses life and rage into our sins, turning them into many devils within us. Like prisoners, they attempt to break free from the prison of our body, seeking to escape through our eyes, mouth, or ears, to the scandal of the gospel, the reproach of religion, the darkening of our evidences, and the damnation of our souls.

But I will say, as I have said before, this has often been the experience of God's people. "There has no temptation overtaken you but such as is common to man; but God is faithful, who will not allow you to be tempted beyond what you are able" (1 Corinthians 10:13). Refer to the Book of Job, the Book of Psalms, and the Book of Lamentations.

Furthermore, remember that Christ Himself was tempted to

blaspheme, to worship the devil, and to take His own life (Matthew 4; Luke 4); temptations worse than which you can hardly encounter. But He was sinless, that is true. And He is your Savior, and that is equally true! Yes, it is also true that by His being tempted, He became the conqueror of the tempter and a helper to those who are tempted (Colossians 2:14-15; Hebrews 2:15; 4:15-16).

Question: But what could be the reason that some who are coming to Christ are so lamentably cast down and buffeted by temptations?

Answer: There may be several reasons.

Some who are coming to Christ cannot be convinced, until temptation arises, that they are as vile as Scripture says they are. It is true that they see enough of their wretchedness to drive them to Christ. However, there is an additional depth of wickedness that they do not perceive. Peter did not realize that he had cursing, swearing, lying, and a tendency in his heart to deny his Master until the temptation came. When that temptation did come upon him, he discovered it to his sorrow (John 13:36-38; Mark 14:36-40; 68-72).

Some who are coming to Jesus Christ are overly focused on their own graces and not sufficiently captivated by the person of Christ. Therefore, God, in order to divert them from being enamored with their own virtues, and to direct their attention more toward the person, work, and merits of His Son, allows them to be cast into the depths of temptation.

This understanding aligns with Job's words: "If I wash myself with snow-water, and make my hands never so clean, yet You will plunge me in the ditch, and my own clothes shall abhor me" (Job 9:30). Job had been a bit too preoccupied with his own graces, elevating his own excellencies too highly, as evidenced by the following texts: Job 33:8-13, 34:5-10, 35:2-3, 38:1-2, 40:10, and 42:3-6. However, by the time the temptations had concluded, you find that he had learned a valuable lesson.

Indeed, God often, for this very reason, seems to take our graces from us, leaving us almost entirely to ourselves and to the tempter, so that we may learn not to love the picture more than the person of His Son. Consider how He dealt with them in Ezekiel 16 and Hosea 2.

Perhaps you have been too quick to judge your brother, condemning him for being a poor, tempted man. God, to humble your pride, allows the tempter to be unleashed upon you, so that you may also feel your own weakness. For "pride goes before destruction, and a haughty spirit before a fall" (Proverbs 16:18).

It may be that you have dealt too harshly with those whom God has wounded in this way, not considering yourself, lest you also be tempted. Therefore, God has allowed this to come upon you (Galatians 6:1).

It may be that you have been given to slumber and sleep, and thus these temptations were sent to awaken you. You know that Peter's temptation came upon him after he had been sleeping; instead of watching and praying, he denied, and denied, and denied his Master (Matthew 26).

It may be that you have presumed too far and relied too much on your own strength, which is why a time of temptation has come upon you. This was also a reason why temptation came upon Peter—he declared, "Though all men forsake You, yet will not I." Ah! That is indeed the way to be tempted (John 13:36-38).

It may be that God intends to make you wise, so that you can speak a word in season to others who are afflicted; therefore, He allows you to be tempted. Christ was tempted so that He might be able to help those who are tempted (Hebrews 2:18).

It may be that Satan has dared God to allow him to tempt you, promising himself that if God permits it, you will curse Him to His face.

Thus, he obtained permission to tempt Job. Therefore, take heed, tempted soul, lest you prove the devil's words true (Job 1:11).

It may be that your graces must be tested in the fire, so that the rust clinging to them may be removed, and they may be proven, both before angels and demons, to be far better than gold that perishes. It may also be that your graces are to receive special praise, honor, and glory at the coming of the Lord Jesus for all the deeds you have accomplished through them against hell and its infernal crew during your time of temptation (1 Peter 1:6, 7).

It may be that God wants others to learn from your sighs, groans, and complaints under temptation, to beware of those sins for which you are currently being delivered to the tormentors.

To conclude this, let us consider the worst-case scenario. Suppose that you are still without the grace of God; you are still a miserable creature, a sinner in need of a blessed Savior. The text presents you with one who is as good and kind as your heart could wish, who also encourages you by saying, "And him who comes to Me I will in no wise cast out."

Now, let us move to a word of application. Is it true that those who are coming to Jesus Christ are often heartily afraid that He will not receive them? This teaches us that faith and doubt can coexist in the same soul. "O you of little faith, why did you doubt?" (Matthew 14:31). He does not say, "O you of no faith!" but rather, "O you of little faith!" because even in the midst of many doubts, there is still a measure of faith.

This is true for many who come to Jesus Christ. They approach with fear, doubting whether they truly come. When they focus on the promise or a word of encouragement by faith, they come; but when they look at themselves or the difficulties ahead, they doubt. "Bid me come," said Peter; "Come," said Christ. So he stepped out of the ship to go to Jesus, but he faced the trial of walking on water.

The same is true for the poor, desiring soul. "Bid me come," says the sinner; "Come," says Christ, "and I will in no wise cast you out." So he comes, but he finds himself facing drowning difficulties. If the winds of temptation blow, the waves of doubt and fear will arise, and this coming sinner will begin to sink if he has but little faith.

However, you will find in Peter's little faith a twofold action: coming and crying. Little faith cannot come all the way without crying. As long as its holy boldness lasts, it can come with peace; but when that boldness fades, it will continue on with cries for help. Peter went as far as his little faith would carry him, and he cried out as far as his little faith would allow, "Lord, save me, I perish!" With both coming and crying, he was kept from sinking, even though he had only a little faith. "Jesus stretched out His hand and caught him, and said to him, 'O you of little faith, why did you doubt?'"

Is it true that those who are coming to Jesus Christ are often heartily afraid that He will not receive them? This reveals the reason for the dejection and despair that we often observe in those who are approaching Jesus Christ. They fear that He will not accept them. The world mocks us for being a dejected people, but they do not understand the cause of our sorrow.

If we could be convinced, even in our dejection, that Jesus Christ would indeed receive us, it would lift us above their mockery and fill our hearts with more joy than when their corn, wine, and oil increase (Psalm 4:6, 7). But it is true that those who are coming to Jesus Christ are often heartily afraid that He will not receive them. This shows that they are awakened, sensitive, and thoughtful individuals.

Fear arises from an awareness and consideration of things. They are aware of their sin, conscious of the curse that is due to it. They are also aware of the glorious majesty of God and what a blessed thing it is to be received by Jesus Christ. They consider the glory of heaven and the evil of sin, and they are sensitive to these realities. "When I remember, I am afraid." "When I consider, I am afraid" (Job 21:6; 23:15).

These thoughts weigh heavily on their spirits, as they are awake and aware. If they were dead like other men, they would not be troubled by fear as they are. Dead men do not fear, feel, or care, but the living and aware person is often heartily afraid that Jesus Christ will not receive him.

The dead and senseless are not distressed. They are presumptuous and groundlessly confident. Who is bolder than the blind? These individuals should indeed fear and be afraid because they are not coming to Jesus Christ. Oh! The hell, the fire, the pit, the wrath of God, and the torment of hell that are prepared for neglectful sinners! "How shall we escape if we neglect so great a salvation?" (Hebrews 3:3). But they lack awareness of these things and therefore cannot fear.

Is it true that those who are coming to Jesus Christ are often heartily afraid that He will not receive them? This should teach older Christians to have compassion and pray for younger seekers. You know the heart of a stranger because you yourselves were once strangers in the land of Egypt. You understand the fears, doubts, and terrors that they experience because you once faced them yourselves.

Therefore, have compassion on them, pray for them, and encourage them; they need all of this. Guilt has overtaken them, and fears of God's wrath have overwhelmed them. Perhaps they are on the brink of hellfire, and the fear of going there burns hot within their hearts. You may know how cunningly Satan suggests his devilish doubts to them, hoping to sink and drown them under the weight of those doubts.

Older Christians, clear the path for them; remove the stumbling blocks from the way, lest the feeble and weak be turned aside, but let them rather be healed (Hebrews 12).

16. Christ Wants No One Who Comes to Fear Rejection

Now, I come to the next observation, which is that Jesus Christ does not want those who are truly coming to Him to ever think that He will cast them out.

The text is full of this: for He says, "And him that comes to Me I will in no wise cast out." Now, if He says, "I will not," He would not have us think that He will. This is further evident by these considerations.

First, Christ Jesus forbids even those who are not yet coming to Him to think of Him in such a way. "Do not think," He said, "that I will accuse you to the Father" (John 5:45).

These individuals, as I mentioned, were not yet coming to Him. For He says of them a little earlier, "And you will not come to Me," because their regard for the honor of men kept them back. Yet, I say, Jesus Christ makes it clear that although He might justly reject them, He would not do so, but instead tells them not to think that He would accuse them to the Father. To not accuse, in Christ's view, is to plead for: for Christ does not stand neutral between the Father and sinners. Therefore, if Jesus Christ does not want them to think that He will accuse those who do not come to Him, then He certainly does not want those who are truly coming to Him to think so either. "And him that comes to Me I will in no wise cast out."

Second, when the woman caught in adultery, even in the very act, was brought before Jesus Christ, He handled the situation with both words and actions in such a way that it was evident He did not come into the world to condemn or cast out. When they set her before Him and charged her with her heinous act, He stooped down and wrote on the ground with His finger, as if He did not hear them. What did He accomplish by this behavior? He plainly testified that He was not in favor of receiving accusations against poor sinners, regardless of who was accusing them.

And observe, even though they continued to ask, thinking they could force Him to condemn her, He answered in a way that drove all the condemning individuals away from her. Then He added, for her encouragement to come to Him, "Neither do I condemn you; go, and sin no more" (John 8:1-11).

This does not mean that He condoned the act; rather, He would not condemn the woman for her sin because that was not His role. He was not sent "into the world to condemn the world, but that the world through Him might be saved" (John 3:17). Now, if Christ, even when urged, would not condemn the guilty woman, who was far from coming to Him, He certainly would not want those who are truly coming to Him to think that He will cast them out. "And him that comes to Me I will in no wise cast out."

Third, Christ plainly invites the turning sinner to come and forbids him from entertaining any thoughts that He will cast him out. "Let the wicked forsake his way, and the unrighteous man his thoughts; and let him return to the Lord, and He will have mercy upon him; and to our God, for He will abundantly pardon" (Isaiah 55:7). The Lord, by urging the unrighteous to forsake his thoughts, specifically forbids those thoughts that hinder the coming person in his progress to Jesus Christ—his unbelieving thoughts.

Therefore, He instructs him not only to forsake his ways but also his thoughts. "Let the wicked forsake his way, and the unrighteous man his thoughts." It is not enough to forsake one if you wish to come to Jesus Christ; because the other will prevent you from doing so. Suppose a man forsakes his wicked ways, his debauched and filthy life; yet if he entertains and nurtures thoughts that Jesus Christ will not receive him, those thoughts will keep him from coming to Jesus Christ.

Sinner, coming sinner, are you willing to come to Jesus Christ? Yes, says the sinner. Then forsake your wicked ways. So I do, says the sinner.

Why do you come so slowly? Because I am hindered. What hinders you? Has God forbidden you? No. Are you not willing to come faster? Yes, yet I cannot. Well, please be honest with me and tell me the reason for your discouragement. The sinner replies, though God does not forbid me, and though I am willing to come faster, there naturally arise these thoughts in my heart that hinder my speed to Jesus Christ. Sometimes I think I am not chosen; sometimes I think I am not called; sometimes I think I have come too late; and sometimes I think I do not know what it is to come. At one moment I think I have no grace; then again, I think I cannot pray; and then I think I am a hypocrite. These thoughts keep me from coming to Jesus Christ.

Look now, did I not tell you so? There are still thoughts remaining in the heart of those who have forsaken their wicked ways; and those thoughts plague them more than anything else because they hinder their coming to Jesus Christ. The sin of unbelief, which is the root of all these thoughts, besets a coming sinner more easily than his ways do (Hebrews 12:1-4). But now, since Jesus Christ commands you to forsake these thoughts, forsake them, coming sinner; and if you do not forsake them, you transgress the commands of Christ, remain your own tormentor, and keep yourself from being established in grace. "If you will not believe, surely you shall not be established" (Isaiah 7:9). Thus you see how Jesus Christ stands against such thoughts that discourage the coming sinner; and thereby truly affirms the doctrine we have in hand: that Jesus Christ would not have those who are truly coming to Him think that He will cast them out. "And him that comes to Me I will in no wise cast out."

17. Reasons for the Observation

I now come to the reasons for the observation.

If Jesus Christ were to allow you to think that He would cast you out, He would also be allowing you to think that He would break His promise. He has said, "I will in no wise cast out." But Christ does not want you to think of Him as one who would break His word; for He declares of Himself, "I am the truth." Therefore, He would not have anyone who is truly coming to Him think that He will cast them out.

If Jesus Christ were to permit the sinner who is genuinely coming to Him to think that He would cast him out, He would be endorsing the first signs of unbelief, which He considers His greatest enemy. He has even directed His holy gospel against it. Therefore, Jesus Christ would not want those who are truly coming to Him to think that He will cast them out. See Matthew 14:31, 21:21, Mark 11:23, Luke 24:25.

If Jesus Christ were to allow the coming sinner to think that He would cast him out, He would also be allowing him to question whether He is willing to receive His Father's gift. The coming sinner is indeed His Father's gift, as the text states. He testifies, "All that the Father gives Me shall come to Me; and him that comes to Me I will in no wise cast out." Therefore, Jesus Christ would not want anyone who is truly coming to Him to think that He will cast them out.

If Jesus Christ were to allow those who are genuinely coming to Him to think that He would cast them out, He would also be allowing them to believe that He would despise and reject the drawing of His Father. No one can come to Him unless the Father draws them. To imagine such a thing would be blasphemous and wicked. Therefore, Jesus Christ would not want anyone who comes to Him to think that He will cast them out.

If Jesus Christ were to allow those who are truly coming to Him to think that He would cast them out, He would also be permitting them to believe that He would be unfaithful to the trust and responsibility that His Father has given Him. His charge is to save, not to lose anything of what He has been given to save (John 6:39). Since the Father has entrusted Him with the task of saving the coming sinner, it cannot be that He would allow such a one to think that He will cast them out.

If Jesus Christ were to allow those who are coming to Him to think that He would cast them out, He would also be allowing them to question His faithfulness in His role as priest. As part of His priestly office, He has paid the price for and redeemed souls, and He continually intercedes with God for those who come (Hebrews 7:25). He cannot permit us to doubt His faithful execution of His priestly duties. Therefore, He cannot allow anyone who is coming to think that they will be cast out.

If Jesus Christ were to allow us to think that the coming sinner would be cast out, He would also be allowing us to question His will, power, or merit to save. But He cannot allow us to question any of these. Therefore, we cannot think that the coming sinner will be cast out. (1) He cannot allow us to question His will; for He says in the text, "I WILL in no wise cast out." (2) He cannot allow us to question His power; for the Holy Spirit says He is able to save to the uttermost those who come. (3) He cannot allow us to question the efficacy of His merit; for the blood of Christ cleanses the one who comes from all sin (1 John 1:7). Therefore, He cannot allow anyone who is coming to Him to think that He will cast them out.

If Jesus Christ were to allow the coming sinner to think that He would cast him out, He would also be allowing him to contradict the clear testimony of the Father, Son, and Spirit, as well as the entire gospel found in Moses, the prophets, the book of Psalms, and what is commonly called the New Testament. But He cannot allow this; therefore, He does not permit the coming sinner to think that He will cast them out.

Lastly, if Jesus Christ were to allow the one who is coming to Him to think that He would cast him out, He would also be allowing him to question His Father's oath, which He has taken in truth and righteousness, so that those who have fled for refuge to Jesus Christ might have strong consolation. But He cannot allow this; therefore, He cannot permit the coming sinner to think that He will cast them out (Hebrews 6).

18. Practical Application

I come now to make some general use and application of the whole, and so to draw towards a conclusion.

The first use is a use of information. First, it informs us that men by nature are far off from Christ. Let me elaborate on this by addressing three questions:

1. Where is he that is coming [but has not come] to Jesus Christ?

2. What is he that is not coming to Jesus Christ?

3. Whither is he to go that cometh not to Jesus Christ?

Where is he?

(1) He is far from God; he is without Him, even alienated from Him in his understanding, will, affections, judgment, and conscience (Ephesians 2:12; 4:18).

(2) He is far from Jesus Christ, who is the only deliverer of men from hellfire (Psalm 73:27).

(3) He is far from the work of the Holy Spirit, the work of regeneration, and a second creation, without which no man shall see the kingdom of heaven (John 3:3).

(4) He is far from the righteousness that should make him acceptable in God's sight (Isaiah 46:12, 13).

(5) He is under the power and dominion of sin; sin reigns in and over him; it dwells in every faculty of his soul and every member of his body, so that from head to foot there is no place clean (Isaiah 1:6; Romans 3:9-18).

(6) He is in the pest-house with Uzziah and excluded from the camp of Israel with the lepers (2 Chronicles 26:21; Numbers 5:2; Job 36:14).

His life is among the unclean. He is in the gall of bitterness and in the bond of iniquity (Acts 8:28).

(7) He is in sin, in the flesh, in death, in the snare of the devil, and is taken captive by him at his will (1 Corinthians 15:17; Romans 8:8; 1 John 3:14; 2 Timothy 2:26).

(8) He is under the curse of the law, and the devil dwells in him and has mastery over him (Galatians 3:13; Ephesians 2:2, 3; Acts 26:18).

(9) He is in darkness, walks in darkness, and knows not whither he goes; for darkness has blinded his eyes.

(10) He is on the broad way that leads to destruction; and if he continues on this path, he will assuredly enter through the broad gate and descend into hell.

What is he that cometh not to Jesus Christ?

(1) He is counted one of God's enemies (Luke 19:14; Romans 8:7).

(2) He is a child of the devil and of hell; for the devil begat him, as to his sinful nature, and hell must swallow him at last because he does not come to Jesus Christ (John 8:44; 1 John 3:8; Matthew 23:15; Psalm 9:17).

(3) He is a child of wrath, an heir of it; it is his portion, and God will repay it to him to his face (Ephesians 2:1-3; Job 21:29-31).

(4) He is a self-murderer; he wrongs his own soul and is one that loves death (Proverbs 1:18; 8:36).

(5) He is a companion for devils and damned men (Proverbs 21:16;

Matthew 25:41).

Whither is he like to go that cometh not to Jesus Christ?

(1) He that cometh not to Him is likely to go further from Him; every sin is a step further from Jesus Christ (Hosea 11).

(2) As he is in darkness, so he is likely to continue in it; for Christ is the light of the world, and he that comes not to Him walks in darkness (John 8:12).

(3) He is likely to be removed at last as far from God, Christ, heaven, and all felicity as an infinite God can remove him (Matthew 12:41).

But, second, this doctrine of coming to Christ informs us where poor destitute sinners may find life for their souls, and that is in Christ. This life is in His Son; he that has the Son has life. And again, "Whoso findeth me findeth life, and shall obtain favor of the Lord" (Proverbs 8:35).

Now, for further enlargement, I will also here propose three more questions:

1. What life is in Christ?

2. Who may have it?

3. Upon what terms?

What life is in Jesus Christ?

(1) There is justifying life in Christ. Man, by sin, is dead in law; and Christ alone can deliver him by His righteousness and blood from this death into a state of life. "For God sent His Son into the world, that we might live through Him" (1 John 4:9). This means through the righteousness He accomplished and the death He died.

(2) There is eternal life in Christ; a life that is endless, a life forever and ever. "He has given us eternal life, and this life is in His Son" (1 John 5:11). Since justification and eternal salvation are both found in Christ and nowhere else, who would not come to Jesus Christ?

Who may have this life?

I answer, poor, helpless, miserable sinners. Specifically,

(1) Those who are willing to have it. "Whosoever will, let him take the water of life" (Revelation 22:17).

(2) Those who thirst for it. "I will give unto him that is athirst of the fountain of the water of life" (Revelation 21:6).

(3) Those who are weary of their sins. "This is the rest with which you may cause the weary to rest; and this is the refreshing" (Isaiah 28:12).

(4) Those who are poor and needy. "He shall spare the poor and needy, and shall save the souls of the needy" (Psalm 72:13).

(5) Those who follow after Him and cry for life. "He who follows Me shall not walk in darkness, but shall have the light of life" (John 8:12).

Upon what terms may he have this life?

(Answer) Freely. Sinner, do you hear? You may have it freely. Let him take the water of life freely. I will give him of the fountain of the water of life freely. "And when they had nothing to pay, he frankly forgave them both" (Luke 7:42). Freely, without money, or without price. "Ho! Everyone who thirsts, come to the waters; and he who has no money, come, buy and eat; yes, come, buy wine and milk without money and without price" (Isaiah 55:1).

Sinner, are you thirsty? Are you weary? Are you willing? Come, then, and do not regard your possessions; for all the good that is in Christ is offered to the coming sinner without money and without price. He has life to give away to those who want it and who do not have a penny to purchase it; and He will give it freely. Oh, what a blessed condition the coming sinner is in!

But, third, this doctrine of coming to Jesus Christ for life informs us that it is to be found nowhere else. If it could be found anywhere else, the text and Him who spoke it would be of little value; for what greater matter is there in "I will in no wise cast out," if another stood by who could receive them? Here appears the glory of Christ, that none but He can save. And here appears His love, that although none can save but He, yet He is not reluctant in saving. "But him that comes to Me," says He, "I will in no wise cast out."

That none can save but Jesus Christ is evident from Acts 4:12: "Neither is there salvation in any other;" and "He has given to us eternal life, and this life is in His Son" (1 John 5:11). If life could have been found anywhere else, it should have been in the law. But it is not in the law; for by the deeds of the law, no man living shall be justified; and if not justified, then no life. Therefore, life is nowhere to be found but in Jesus Christ (Galatians 3).

(Question) But why would God arrange it so that life should be found nowhere else but in Jesus Christ?

(Answer) There is reason for it, both with respect to God and to us.

With respect to God.

(1) It is necessary for life to be found in a way that reflects both justice and mercy. It could not be just if it were not through Christ, for He alone was able to fulfill the demands of the law and provide what justice required for sin. If the curse for our sins had been placed upon the angels, they would have been condemned to hell forever. However, that curse was placed upon Jesus Christ, who bore it, satisfied the

penalty, and redeemed His people from it. Now, God Himself proclaims that He is faithful and just to forgive us if we come to Jesus in faith and trust in what He has done for our life (Romans 3:24-26; John 1:4).

(2) Life must come through Jesus Christ so that God may be adored and magnified for revealing this way. This is the Lord's doing, so that in all things He might be glorified through Jesus Christ our Lord.

(3) Life must be found in Jesus Christ so that it may be at God's disposal, who has great compassion for the poor, the lowly, the meek, the brokenhearted, and for those whom others neglect (Psalm 34:6; 138:6; 25:51:17; 147:3).

(4) Life must be in Christ to eliminate any boasting from the lips of men. This is also the apostle's reasoning in Romans 3:19, 27 (Ephesians 2:8-10).

Life must be in Jesus Christ with respect to us.

1. That we might have it on the easiest terms, namely, freely: as a gift, not as wages. If it were in Moses' hands, we would struggle to obtain it. If it were in the pope's hands, we would have to pay dearly for it. But thanks be to God, it is in Christ, laid up in Him, and communicated to sinners on easy terms—simply by receiving, accepting, and embracing it with thanksgiving, as the Scriptures clearly declare (John 1:11, 12; 2 Corinthians 11:4; Hebrews 11:13; Colossians 3:13-15).

2. Life is in Christ for us, so that it is not built on such a fragile foundation as it would be if it were anywhere else. The law itself is weak because of us in this regard. But Christ is a tried stone, a sure foundation—one who will not fail to bear your burden and receive your soul, O coming sinner.

3. Life is in Christ so that it might be sure to all the seed. Alas! If life were left in our hands, we would surely forfeit it over and over again.

If it were in any other hands, our frequent backslidings would offend Him so greatly that He would eventually shut His bowels of compassion against us forever. But now it is in Christ, with one who can pity, pray for, pardon, and even multiply pardons. It is with one who can have compassion on us when we stray, who has a heart to bring us back when we go astray, and who can pardon without reproach. Blessed be God that life is in Christ! For now it is sure to all the seed.

4. This doctrine of coming to Jesus Christ for life informs us of the evil of unbelief—the wicked thing that is the primary hindrance for the coming sinner. Does the text say, "Come?" Does it say, "And him who comes to me I will in no wise cast out?" Then what an evil it is that keeps sinners from coming to Jesus Christ! That evil is unbelief; for by faith we come, and by unbelief we stay away. Therefore, it is said to be that by which a soul departs from God, as it was the very thing that caused the world to turn away from Him, and it continues to keep them from Him to this day. It does so all the more easily because it does so with cunning.

The Sin of Unbelief - This sin may be called the white devil, for it often appears in its mischievous workings in the soul as if it were an angel of light; indeed, it acts like a counselor from heaven. Therefore, let us briefly discuss this evil disease.

It is that sin, above all others, that has some semblance of reason in its attempts. It keeps the soul from Christ by pretending that it is currently unfit and unprepared; it claims a lack of sufficient awareness of sin, a lack of repentance, a lack of humility, and a lack of a broken heart.

It is the sin that most aligns with the conscience. The conscience of the coming sinner tells him that he has nothing good; that he stands guilty for ten thousand talents; that he is a very ignorant, blind, and hard-hearted sinner, unworthy of even being noticed by Jesus Christ. And will you, says Unbelief, in such a state as you are now, presume to come to Jesus Christ?

It is the sin that most resonates with our sense of feeling. The coming sinner feels the workings of sin, of all kinds of sin and wretchedness in his flesh; he also feels the wrath and judgment of God due to sin, and often staggers under it. Now, says Unbelief, you see you have no grace; for what works in you is corruption. You may also perceive that God does not love you because the sense of His wrath remains upon you. Therefore, how can you dare to come to Jesus Christ?

It is that sin, above all others, that most aligns with the wisdom of our flesh. The wisdom of our flesh thinks it prudent to hesitate, to hold back for a while, to listen to both sides for a time, and not to be rash, sudden, or unadvised in too boldly presuming upon Jesus Christ. And this wisdom is where unbelief finds its footing.

It is that sin which continually whispers in the soul's ear with doubts about the faithfulness of God in keeping His promises to those who come to Jesus Christ for life. It also suggests mistrust regarding Christ's willingness to receive and save. No sin can do this as subtly as unbelief.

It is also that sin which is always ready to raise objections against this or that promise that the Spirit of God brings to our hearts to comfort us. If the poor coming sinner is not vigilant, it will, through some evasion, slight, trick, or cavil, quickly wrest the promise away from him, leaving him with little benefit from it.

It is that sin, above all others, that weakens our prayers, our faith, our love, our diligence, our hope, and our expectations. It even takes the heart away from God in duty.

Lastly, this sin, as I have just mentioned, appears in the soul with so many enticing pretenses of safety and security that it seems like counsel sent from heaven. It advises the soul to be wise, cautious, considerate, and well-advised, urging it to avoid too hasty a leap into believing.

Be sure, first, that God loves you; do not grasp any promise until you are compelled by God to do so. Do not be confident in your salvation; continue to doubt it, even though the testimony of the Lord has been frequently confirmed in you.

Do not live by faith, but by your senses; and when you cannot see or feel, then let fear and mistrust take hold, leading you to doubt and question everything. This is the devilish counsel of unbelief, so cloaked in appealing pretenses that even the wisest Christian can hardly shake off these reasonings.

But to be brief, let me provide you, Christian reader, with a more detailed description of the qualities of unbelief by contrasting it with faith in these twenty-five particulars:

1. Faith believes the Word of God; but unbelief questions its certainty (Psalm 106:24).

2. Faith believes the Word because it is true; but unbelief doubts it because it is true (1 Timothy 4:3; John 8:45).

3. Faith sees more in a promise of God to help than in all other things that hinder; but unbelief, despite God's promise, says, "How can these things be?" (Romans 4:19-21; 2 Kings 7:2; John 3:11,12).

4. Faith will make you see love in the heart of Christ, even when He gives reproofs with His mouth; but unbelief will imagine wrath in His heart, even when He speaks and declares His love for us (Matthew 15:22,28; Numbers 13; 2 Chronicles 14:3).

5. Faith helps the soul to wait, even when God delays in giving; but unbelief will become upset and abandon everything if God takes any time (Psalm 25:5; Isaiah 8:17; 2 Kings 6:33; Psalm 106:13,14).

6. Faith provides comfort in the midst of fears; but unbelief creates fears in the midst of comfort (2 Chronicles 20:20,21; Matthew 8:26; Luke 24:26,27).

7. Faith will draw sweetness from God's rod; but unbelief finds no comfort in His greatest mercies (Psalm 23:4; Numbers 21).

8. Faith makes great burdens light; but unbelief makes light burdens intolerably heavy (2 Corinthians 4:1; 14-18; Malachi 1:12,13).

9. Faith helps us when we are down; but unbelief brings us down when we are up (Micah 7:8-10; Hebrews 4:11).

Faith brings us near to God when we are far from Him; but unbelief puts us far from God when we are near to Him (Hebrews 10:22; 3:12,13).

Where faith reigns, it declares men to be the friends of God; but where unbelief reigns, it declares them to be His enemies (John 3:23; Hebrews 3:18; Revelation 21:8).

Faith places a person under grace; but unbelief keeps him under wrath (Romans 3:24-26; 14:6; Ephesians 2:8; John 3:36; 1 John 5:10; Hebrews 3:17; Mark 16:16).

Faith purifies the heart; but unbelief keeps it polluted and impure (Acts 15:9; Titus 1:15,16).

By faith, the righteousness of Christ is credited to us; but through unbelief, we are confined under the law and destined to perish (Romans 4:23-24; 11:32; Galatians 3:23).

Faith makes our work acceptable to God through Christ; but anything that comes from unbelief is sin. For without faith, it is impossible to please Him (Hebrews 11:4; Romans 14:23; Hebrews 6:6).

Faith gives us peace and comfort in our souls; but unbelief causes trouble and turmoil, like the restless waves of the sea (Romans 5:1; James 1:6).

Faith allows us to see the preciousness of Christ; but unbelief perceives no form, beauty, or attractiveness in Him (1 Peter 2:7; Isaiah 53:2-3).

By faith, we have our life in the fullness of Christ; but through unbelief, we starve and wither away (Galatians 2:20).

Faith grants us victory over the law, sin, death, the devil, and all evils; but unbelief leaves us vulnerable to them all (1 John 5:4-5; Luke 12:46).

Faith reveals to us greater excellence in things not seen than in those that are visible; but unbelief sees more in the things that are seen than in the things that will be in the future (2 Corinthians 4:18; Hebrews 11:24-27; 1 Corinthians 15:32).

Faith makes the ways of God pleasant and admirable; but unbelief makes them burdensome and difficult (Galatians 5:6; 1 Corinthians 12:10-11; John 6:60; Psalm 2:3).

By faith, Abraham, Isaac, and Jacob inherited the land of promise; but due to unbelief, neither Aaron, nor Moses, nor Miriam could enter it (Hebrews 11:9; 3:19).

By faith, the children of Israel crossed through the Red Sea; but because of unbelief, the majority of them perished in the wilderness (Hebrews 11:29; Jude 5).

By faith, Gideon accomplished more with three hundred men and a few empty pitchers than all twelve tribes could achieve because they did not believe God (Judges 7:16-22; Numbers 14:11-14).

By faith, Peter walked on the water; but through unbelief, he began to sink (Matthew 14:28-30).

Many more examples could be added, which I omit for brevity's sake. I urge everyone who believes they have a soul to save or to lose to take heed of unbelief. Let us not, seeing that there is a promise left to us of entering into His rest, fall short of it through unbelief.

The second use is a use of examination. Sinner, you have heard of the necessity of coming to Christ, the willingness of Christ to receive the soul that comes to Him, and the benefits that those who truly come to Him will receive. Now, I urge you to seriously inquire: Have I truly come to Jesus Christ?

I could present many motives to encourage you to sincerely perform this duty. For example:

1. You are in sin, in the flesh, in death, ensnared by the devil, and under the curse of the law if you are not coming to Jesus Christ.

2. There is no way to be delivered from these conditions except by coming to Jesus Christ.

3. If you come, Jesus Christ will receive you and will not cast you out.

4. You will not regret it on the day of judgment if you come to Jesus Christ now.

5. However, you will surely mourn in the end if you refuse to come now.

6. Lastly, now that you have been invited to come, your judgment will be greater and your damnation more severe if you refuse than if you had never heard of coming to Christ.

Objection: But we hope we have come to Jesus Christ.

Answer: It is good if it proves to be so. However, to avoid speaking without basis and inadvertently falling into hellfire, let us examine this matter a little more closely.

First, have you truly come to Jesus Christ? What have you left behind? What did you turn away from in your coming to Jesus Christ?

When Lot left Sodom, he left the Sodomites behind him (Genesis 19). When Abraham departed from Chaldea, he left his country and relatives behind him (Genesis 12; Acts 7). When Ruth came to trust under the wings of the Lord God of Israel, she left her father and mother, her gods, and the land of her birth behind her (Ruth 1:15-17; 2:11,12). When Peter came to Christ, he left his nets behind him (Matthew 4:20). When Zacchaeus came to Christ, he left the tax collector's booth behind him (Luke 19). When Paul came to Christ, he left his own righteousness behind him (Philippians 3:7,8). When those who practiced magic came to Jesus Christ, they took their curious books and burned them, even though they were valued at fifty thousand pieces of silver in another's eyes (Acts 19:18-20).

What do you say, friend? Have you left behind your cherished sins, your sinful pleasures, your vain companions, your unlawful gains, your idol-gods, your self-righteousness, and your unlawful practices? If any of these remain with you, and you with them in your heart and life, then you have not yet come to Jesus Christ.

Second, have you come to Jesus Christ? Please tell me what motivated you to come to Him.

People do not usually go to a place without a motivating cause. Likewise, they do not come to Jesus Christ without a cause that moves them to do so. What do you say? Do you have a cause that compels you to come? Being in a state of condemnation is a sufficient reason for anyone to seek life in Jesus Christ. However, that reason will not suffice unless it moves you; and it will not move you until your eyes are opened to see your condition. It is not merely being under wrath that motivates a person to come to Jesus Christ, but the realization of it. Alas! All people are under wrath because of sin, yet few of them come to Jesus Christ. The reason is that they do not see their condition. "Who warned you to flee from the wrath to come?" (Matthew 3:7). Until people are warned and accept the warning, they will not come to Jesus Christ.

Consider three or four examples of this. Adam and Eve did not come to Jesus Christ until they received the alarm and conviction of their lost state due to sin (Genesis 3). The children of Israel did not cry out for a mediator until they recognized their danger of death by the law (Exodus 20:18,19). The publican did not come until he saw himself as lost and undone (Luke 18:13). The prodigal son did not come until he realized death was imminent (Luke 15:17,18). The three thousand did not come until they were unsure of how to be saved (Acts 2:37-39). Paul did not come until he recognized his lost state (Acts 9:3-8,11). Lastly, the jailer did not come until he saw himself as undone (Acts 16:29-31). I tell you, it is easier to persuade a healthy person to visit a physician for a cure, or someone without injury to seek a bandage, than it is to convince someone who does not see their soul's disease to come to Jesus Christ. The healthy have no need of a physician; why should they go to Him? The full pitcher can hold no more; why should it go to the fountain? If you come full, you do not come rightly, and be assured that Christ will send you away empty. "But He heals the brokenhearted and binds up their wounds" (Mark 2:17; Psalm 147:3; Luke 1:53).

Third, are you coming to Jesus Christ? Please tell me, what do you see in Him that draws you to forsake all the world and come to Him?

I ask you, what have you seen in Him? People must perceive something in Jesus Christ; otherwise, they will not come to Him. 1. What beauty have you seen in His person? You will not come if you see no form or beauty in Him (Isaiah 53:1-3). 2. Until those mentioned in the Song were convinced that there was more beauty, charm, and desirability in Christ than in ten thousand others, they did not even inquire where He was, nor did they turn aside to follow Him (Song of Solomon 5, 6).

There are many things in this world that can and do captivate the heart. They will continue to do so as long as you remain blind and are not allowed to see the beauty of the Lord Jesus.

Fourth, have you come to the Lord Jesus? What have you found in Him since you came to Him?

Peter found in Him the word of eternal life (John 6:68). Those whom Peter mentions found Him to be a living stone, one that communicated life to them (1 Peter 2:4, 5). He Himself says that those who come to Him shall find rest for their souls; have you found rest in Him for your soul? (Matthew 11:28).

Let us return to the times of the Old Testament.

Abraham found something in Him that made him leave his country and become a pilgrim and stranger on the earth for His sake (Genesis 12; Hebrews 11).

Moses found something in Him that made him forsake a crown and a kingdom for His sake as well.

David found so much in Him that he counted one day in His house to be better than a thousand elsewhere; indeed, to be a doorkeeper in His house was better, in his estimation, than to dwell in the tents of wickedness (Psalm 84:10).

What did Daniel and the three young men find in Him that made them brave the hazards of the fiery furnace and the den of lions for His sake? (Daniel 3, 6).

Let us turn our attention to the martyrs.

Stephen found something in Him that made him joyful and willing to yield up his life for His name (Acts 7).

Ignatius found something in Christ that made him choose to endure the torments of the devil and hell itself rather than be without Him. -

Fox's Acts and Monuments, vol. 1, p. 52, Anno. 111. Edit. 1632.

What did Romanus see in Christ when he said to the raging Emperor, who threatened him with terrible torments, "Your sentence, O Emperor, I joyfully embrace, and I will not refuse to be sacrificed by whatever cruel torments you can invent?" - Fox, vol. 1, p. 116.

What did Menas, the Egyptian, see in Christ when he said, under the most cruel torments, "There is nothing in my mind that can be compared to the kingdom of heaven; neither is all the world, if it were weighed in a balance, worth more than the price of one soul? Who is able to separate us from the love of Jesus Christ our Lord? I have learned from my Lord and King not to fear those who kill the body," etc. - p. 117.

What did Eulalia see in Christ when she said, as they were pulling her apart, "Behold, O Lord, I will not forget you. What a pleasure it is for them, O Christ, who remember your triumphant victory?" - p. 121.

What do you think Agnes saw in Christ when she joyfully went to meet the soldier appointed to be her executioner? "I will willingly," she said, "receive this sword into my breast, drawing its force even to the hilt; that thus, being married to Christ my spouse, I may overcome and escape all the darkness of this world." - p. 122.

What do you think Julitta saw in Christ when, upon the Emperor's warning that unless she worshipped the gods, she would never have protection, laws, judgments, or life, she replied, "Farewell life, welcome death; farewell riches, welcome poverty! All that I have, even if it were a thousand times more, I would rather lose than speak one wicked and blasphemous word against my Creator." - p. 123.

What did Marcus Arethusius see in Christ when, after his enemies had cut his flesh, anointed it with honey, and hung him up in a basket for flies and bees to feed on, he refused to give even a halfpenny to uphold idolatry in order to save his life? - p. 128.

What did Constantine see in Christ when he would kiss the wounds of those who suffered for him? - p. 135.

But what need is there to provide such particular instances of words and smaller actions? Their lives, their blood, their enduring hunger, sword, fire, being pulled apart, and all the torments that the devil and hell could devise, all testify to the love they bore for Christ after they had come to Him.

What have YOU found in Him, sinner?

What! Come to Christ and find nothing in Him! When all things worth seeking are found in Him! Or if you find anything, is it not enough to wean you from your sinful delights and fleshly lusts? Away, away! You are not truly coming to Jesus Christ.

He who has come to Jesus Christ has found in Him what cannot be found anywhere else. He has found God reconciling the world to Himself, not counting their trespasses against them. Therefore, God is not to be found in heaven or on earth besides Him (2 Corinthians 5:19-20).

He who has come to Jesus Christ has found in Him a fountain of grace, sufficient not only to pardon sin but also to sanctify the soul and to preserve it from falling in this evil world.

He who has come to Jesus Christ has found virtue in Him; that virtue which, if He touches you with His Word, or if you touch Him by faith, life is immediately conveyed into your soul. It awakens you as one who has been roused from sleep; it stirs all the powers of the soul (Psalm 30:11-12; Song of Solomon 6:12).

Have you come to Jesus Christ? You have found glory in Him, a glory that surpasses all else. "You are more glorious than the mountains of prey" (Psalm 76:4).

What can I say? You have found righteousness in Him; you have found rest, peace, delight, heaven, glory, and eternal life.

Sinner, take heed; ask your heart again, saying, "Have I come to Jesus Christ?" For upon this one question—whether you have come or not—hangs heaven and hell for you. If you can say, "I have come," and God approves of that statement, then happy, happy, happy are you! But if you have not come, what can make you happy? What can bring happiness to one who, by not coming to Jesus Christ for life, must be damned in hell?

The third use - A use of encouragement. Coming sinner, I have a word for you; be of good comfort, "He will in no wise cast out." Of all men, you are the blessed of the Lord; the Father has prepared His Son to be a sacrifice for you, and Jesus Christ, your Lord, has gone to prepare a place for you (John 1:29; Hebrews 10). What shall I say to you?

First, you come to a full Christ; you will lack nothing for your soul or body, for this world or the next, as everything you need can be found in or through Jesus Christ. Just as it was said of the land that the Danites went to possess, so, with even more truth, it can be said of Christ: He is the one with whom there is no lack of any good thing that is in heaven or on earth. A full Christ is your Christ.

He is full of grace. Grace is sometimes understood as love; no one has ever loved like Jesus Christ. Jonathan's love surpassed that of women, but the love of Christ surpasses all knowledge. It is beyond the love of all the earth, of all creatures, even of men and angels. His love compelled Him to lay aside His glory, to leave the heavenly realm, to clothe Himself in flesh, to be born in a stable, to be laid in a manger, to live a life of poverty in this world, to take upon Himself our sicknesses, infirmities, sins, curses, death, and the wrath due to man. And all this He did for a base, undeserving, ungrateful people; indeed, for a people who were at enmity with Him. "For when we were still without strength, in due time Christ died for the ungodly. For scarcely for a righteous man will one die; yet perhaps for a good man someone would even dare to die. But God demonstrates His own love toward us, in that while we were still sinners, Christ died for us. Much more then, having now been justified by His blood, we shall be saved from wrath through Him. For if when we were enemies we were reconciled to God through the death of His Son, much more, having been reconciled, we shall be saved by His life" (Romans 5:6-10).

He is full of truth. He is full of grace and truth. Truth, that is, faithfulness in keeping promises, including this promise from the text: "I will in no wise cast out" (John 14:6). Hence, it is said that His words are true, and that He is the faithful God who keeps covenant. His promises are called truth: "You will fulfill Your truth to Jacob, and Your mercy to Abraham, which You have sworn to our fathers from the days of old." Therefore, it is said again that both He Himself and His words are truth: "I am the truth, the Scripture of truth" (Daniel 10:21). "Your word is truth" (John 17:17; 2 Samuel 7:28); "Your law is truth" (Psalm 119:142); and "My mouth," says He, "shall speak truth" (Proverbs 8:7). See also Ecclesiastes 12:10, Isaiah 25:1, Malachi 2:6, Acts 26:25, 2 Timothy 2:12-13. Now, I say, His word is truth, and He is full of truth to fulfill His truth even to a thousand generations. Coming sinner, He will not deceive you; come boldly to Jesus Christ.

He is full of wisdom. He has been made wisdom for us by God; wisdom to manage the affairs of His church in general, and the affairs of every coming sinner in particular. For this reason, He is called "head over all things" (1 Corinthians 1; Ephesians 1), because He governs all things in the world by His wisdom for the benefit of His church. All human actions, all of Satan's temptations, all of God's providences, all trials and disappointments—everything is under the authority of Christ, who is the wisdom of God. He orders all things for the good of His church. And rest assured, nothing will happen in the world that will not ultimately serve a good purpose for His church and people, despite any opposition.

He is full of the Spirit, ready to share it with the coming sinner. He has received the Spirit without measure so that He may distribute it to every member of His body, according to the measure allotted to each by the Father. Therefore, He says that whoever comes to Him, "Out of his belly shall flow rivers of living water" (John 3:34; Titus 3:5-6; Acts 2; John 7:33-39).

He is indeed a storehouse filled with all the graces of the Spirit. "Of His fullness we have all received, and grace for grace" (John 1:16). Here is an abundance of faith, love, sincerity, humility, and every other grace; and He gives even more of these to every humble, lowly, penitent coming sinner. Therefore, coming soul, you do not approach a barren wilderness when you come to Jesus Christ.

He is full of compassion and mercy, and those who come to Him for life will surely experience it. He can bear with your weaknesses, He can understand your ignorance, and He can empathize with your infirmities. He can affectionately forgive your transgressions, heal your backslidings, and love you freely. His compassion does not fail; "He will not break a bruised reed, nor quench the smoking flax; He can pity those whom no one else pities, and He is afflicted in all your afflictions" (Matthew 26:41; Hebrews 5:2; 2:18; Matthew 9:2; Hosea 14:4; Ezekiel 16:5-6; Isaiah 63:9; Psalm 78:38; 86:15; 111:4; 112:4; Lamentations 3:22; Isaiah 42:3).

Coming soul, the Jesus to whom you are coming is full of might and power for your benefit; He can suppress all your enemies. He is the Prince of the kings of the earth; He can bend all men's plans for your assistance. He can break every snare laid for you along the way; He can lift you out of all difficulties that surround you. He is wise in heart and mighty in power. Every life under heaven is in His hands; even the fallen angels tremble before Him. And He will save your life, coming sinner (1 Corinthians 1:24; Romans 8:28; Matthew 28:18; Revelation 4; Psalm 19:3; 27:5-6; Job 9:4; John 17:2; Matthew 8:29; Luke 8:28; James 2:19).

Coming sinner, the Jesus to whom you are coming is lowly in heart; He does not despise anyone. It is not your outward poverty, nor your inward weakness; it is not because you are poor, base, deformed, or foolish that He will reject you. He has chosen the foolish, the base, and the despised things of this world to confound the wise and mighty. He will listen to your stammering prayers; He will discern the meaning of your inexpressible groans. He will accept your weakest offering, as long as it comes from your heart (Matthew 11:20; Luke 14:21; Proverbs 9:4-6; Isaiah 38:14-15; Song of Solomon 5:15; John 4:27; Mark 12:33-34; James 5:11). Now, is not this a blessed Christ, coming sinner? Are you not likely to fare well when you embrace Him?

But, secondly, you have yet another advantage in coming to Jesus Christ: He is not only full, but also FREE. He does not withhold what He has; He is open-hearted and generous. Let me illustrate this in a few particulars:

This is evident because He calls you; He invites you to come to Him. He would not do this if He were not free to give. Indeed, He encourages you to ask, seek, and knock. To further encourage you, He adds a promise to every command: "Seek, and you shall find; ask, and you shall have; knock, and it shall be opened to you." If a rich man were to say this to a poor person, would he not be considered generous? If he said to the poor, "Come to my door, ask at my door, knock at my door, and you shall find and receive," would he not be regarded as liberal? Well, this is exactly what Jesus Christ does. Pay attention, coming sinner (Isaiah 55:3; Psalm 50:15; Matthew 7:7-9).

He does not only invite you to come, but He assures you that He will genuinely do you good; indeed, He will do it with joy: "I will rejoice over them to do them good — with My whole heart and with My whole soul" (Jeremiah 32:41).

It is clear that He is free because He gives without reproach. "He gives to all men liberally, and does not upbraid" (James 1:5). There are some who may grant the poor a favor, but they mix their kindness with so many reproaches that the recipients find little joy in it. But Christ does not do so, coming sinner; He casts all your iniquities behind His back (Isaiah 38:17). Your sins and iniquities He will remember no more (Hebrews 8:12).

That Christ is free is evident from the complaints He makes against those who refuse to come to Him for mercy. He laments, saying, "O Jerusalem, Jerusalem! How often would I have gathered your children together, as a hen gathers her chicks under her wings, but you were not willing!" (Matthew 23:37). He expresses this as a complaint. He also says in another place, "But you have not called upon Me, O Jacob" (Isaiah 43:22). Coming sinner, see here the willingness of Christ to save; see here how freely He offers life and all good things to those like you. He complains when you do not come; He is displeased when you do not call upon Him. Listen, coming sinner, once again; when Jerusalem refused to come to Him for safety, "He beheld the city and wept over it, saying, 'If you had known, even you, especially in this your day, the things that belong to your peace! But now they are hidden from your eyes'" (Luke 19:41-42).

Lastly, He is open and generous in His desire to do you good, as seen in the joy and celebration He displays at the return of lost prodigals. He receives the lost sheep with joy, the lost goat with joy; indeed, when the prodigal returned home, what joy and merriment, what music and dancing filled his father's house! (Luke 15).

Thirdly, coming sinner, I will add another encouragement for your help.

God has prepared a mercy seat, a throne of grace for you to approach; so that you may come to Him, and He may hear you and receive you from there. "I will commune with you," He says, "from above the mercy seat" (Exodus 25:22). In other words, sinner, when you come to me, you will find me upon the mercy seat, where I am always found by the desperate coming sinner. There I bring my pardons; there I hear and receive their petitions, and accept them with favor.

God has also prepared a golden altar for you to offer your prayers and tears upon. A golden altar! It is called a "golden altar" to signify its worth in God's eyes; for this golden altar is Jesus Christ. This altar sanctifies your gift and makes your sacrifice acceptable. Therefore, this altar transforms your groans into golden groans; your tears into golden tears; and your prayers into golden prayers, in the sight of the God you approach, coming sinner (Revelation 8; Matthew 23:19; Hebrews 10:10; 1 Peter 2:5).

God has strewn the entire path, from the gate of hell, where you were, to the gate of heaven, where you are going, with flowers from His own garden. Behold how the promises, invitations, calls, and encouragements, like lilies, lie all around you! Take care not to trample them underfoot, sinner. With promises, did I say? Yes, He has mixed all these with His own name, His Son's name; also with the names of mercy, goodness, compassion, love, pity, grace, forgiveness, pardon, and anything else that may encourage the coming sinner.

He has also laid up the names and recorded the sins of those who have been saved for your encouragement. In this book, they are clearly written, so that you, through patience and comfort from the Scriptures, might have hope.

1. In this book is recorded Noah's faults and sins, and how God had mercy upon him.

2. In this record is clearly written the name of Lot, along with the nature of his sin, and how the Lord had mercy upon him.

3. In this record, you will also find the names of Moses, Aaron, Gideon, Samson, David, Solomon, Peter, Paul, along with the nature of their sins, and how God had mercy upon them; all to encourage you, coming sinner.

Fourthly, I will add yet another encouragement for the person coming to Jesus Christ. Are you coming? Are you truly coming? Then know that your coming is by virtue of God's call. You are called. Calling precedes coming. Coming is not of works, but of Him who calls. "He went up into a mountain and called to Him those He wanted; and they came to Him" (Mark 3:13).

Are you coming? This is also due to illumination. God has opened your eyes, and therefore you are coming. As long as you were in darkness, you loved darkness and could not bear to come, because your deeds were evil. But now, having been illuminated and made to see what and where you are, and also what and where your Savior is, you are coming to Jesus Christ. "Blessed are you, Simon Bar-Jonah, for flesh and blood has not revealed this to you, but My Father who is in heaven" (Matthew 16:17).

Are you coming? This is because God has inclined your heart to come. God has called you, illuminated you, and inclined your heart to come; and therefore, you come to Jesus Christ. It is God who works in you to will and to come to Jesus Christ. Coming sinner, bless God for giving you a will to come to Jesus Christ. It is a sign that you belong to Jesus Christ because God has made you willing to come to Him (Psalm 110:3). Bless God for removing the enmity of your mind; had He not done so, you would still hate your own salvation.

Are you coming to Jesus Christ? It is God who gives you power: the power to pursue your will in matters of salvation is a gift from God. "It is God who works in you both to will and to do" (Philippians 2:13). Not that God works the will to come where He gives no power; but you should take note that power is an additional mercy. The church recognized that will and power are two different things when she cried, "Draw me, and we will run after You" (Song of Solomon 1:4). David also understood this when he said, "I will run the way of Your commandments, when You shall enlarge my heart" (Psalm 119:32). The will to come and the power to pursue that will is a double mercy, coming sinner.

All your strange, passionate, and sudden urges to pursue Jesus

Christ—coming sinner, you know what I mean—are also helps from God. Perhaps at times you feel stronger stirrings in your heart to flee to Jesus Christ. Right now, you may be experiencing a sweet and powerful breeze from the Spirit of God, filling your sails with the fresh winds of His good Spirit. During these moments, you ride as if on the wings of the wind, carried beyond yourself, beyond your most fervent prayers, and above all your fears and temptations.

Coming sinner, have you not occasionally felt a kiss from the sweet lips of Jesus Christ? I mean, have you not received some blessed word that drops like honeycomb upon your soul to revive you when you are in the depths of despair?

Does Jesus Christ not sometimes grant you a glimpse of Himself, even if you do not see Him for long—perhaps just as long as it takes to tell twenty?

Have you not sometimes felt as if the very warmth of His wings was overshadowing your soul? This warmth brings a joy to your spirit, much like the bright beams of the sun shining upon your body when it suddenly breaks through the clouds, even if that light is fleeting.

All these experiences are the good hand of your God upon you. They are meant to compel, provoke, and make you willing and able to come, coming sinner, so that in the end, you might be saved.

Made in United States
North Haven, CT
30 July 2025